# PETER PAN, THE LOST CHILD

# PETER PAN, THE LOST CHILD

*Kathleen Kelley-Lainé*

PHOENIX
PUBLISHING HOUSE
*firing the mind*

First published in 1992 in French as *Peter Pan ou l'enfant triste* by Calmann-Lévy

First published in English in 1997 as *Peter Pan: The Story of Lost Childhood* by Element Books

New English translation published in 2023 by
Phoenix Publishing House Ltd
62 Bucknell Road
Bicester
Oxfordshire OX26 2DS

Translated by Kathleen Kelley-Lainé




British Library Cataloguing in Publication Data

A C.I.P. for this book is available from the British Library

ISBN-13: 978-1-91269-130-2

Typeset by vPrompt eServices Pvt Ltd, India

Printed in the United Kingdom

www.firingthemind.com

# Contents

# Author's note

This book has been written using the story of Peter Pan (*Peter Pan in Kensington Gardens* and *Peter Pan*) as its framework. The text consists of material either directly quoted or reworded from J. M. Barrie's classic work, and as such each instance is not individually cited. In the chapters concerning the life of J. M. Barrie, a number of direct quotes are taken from his *Collected Works* and additional material is drawn from Andrew Birkin's biography. Discussions of Freud's life and work are taken from two sources. These are all listed in the Bibliography.

# About the author

**Kathleen Kelley-Lainé** is a trilingual psychoanalyst working in private practice in Paris (in English, French, and Hungarian). She is an active member of the Société Psychanalytique de Paris, the European Psychoanalytical Federation, the International Psychoanalytical Association, and the International Sándor Ferenczi Society. She is internationally known for her many conferences and published articles in psychoanalytical journals and books. Her most well-known book published in French, *Peter Pan ou l'enfant triste,* was translated into English, Hungarian, and Greek and has been in circulation since 1992.

She was born in Budapest, Hungary. Shortly after the war, she and her family fled the Stalinist Regime along with hundreds of post-war refugees. They settled in Toronto, Canada, where Kathleen grew up and was educated in the Ontario Public School System, and continued her studies at the University of Toronto in Sociology, obtaining a master's degree. She began her professional career as lecturer in Sociology at Bishop's University, Quebec, then continued for a number of years in Geneva, Switzerland, for the Geneva Department of Education, participating in the design and creation of a Research and Development Centre for Educational Television. A major part of her career as a sociologist was with the OECD, Centre for Educational Research and Innovation in Paris.

She trained as a psychoanalyst with the Paris Psychoanalytical Society (Société Psychanalytique de Paris). Among her mentors were Drs André Green, Serge Lebovici, René Diatkine, and Janine Chasseguet-Smirgel. As a Member of the Society she was on the Editorial Board of the *Review Française de Psychanalyse*, the Admissions Committee for new candidates. In 2001, she organised the International Psychoanalytical Conference on Immigration and the Loss of the Mother Tongue: UNESCO 'Une Mère, Une Terre, Une Langue' (articles published in *Lost Childhood and the Language of Exile*, Phoenix, 2022).

# Foreword

*Jonathan Sklar*

This is a marvellous book! The author's deconstruction of the personage 'Peter Pan' reveals not only the adventures but also the profound trials and tribulations of a child-adult who has chosen to live in Neverland rather than confront the limits of reality. Three stories intermingle, versions of Peter Pan, the biography of James Matthew Barrie, and extracts from the life of the author-psychoanalyst. Through the interlacing of these story lines, one is gradually led from the 'great adventure' of the 'young, innocent and heartless boy' smiling with his baby teeth, to the vortex of childhood trauma.

The reader is buffeted by intense yearning, wells of desire, and pain, discovering the emotional consequences of life lived in the shadows of tragedy. At times the simple prose reminds us of the hidden flair of Saint-Exupéry's *Le Petit Prince*. As 'little wisdoms' emerge, we, the reader, are surprised to encounter our own children, our own parents, and even ourselves as children with the tribulations of 'growing up'.

Time is that of the psyche, of free association moving backwards and forwards. The story of Peter Pan intermingles with vignettes from the author's psychoanalytic practice as well as from her own wounded childhood. This is a brave book to write, as it is to read. The light innocent story, full of adventures through the eyes of Peter Pan, darkens as we discover the hidden secrets of James Matthew Barrie and how he is condemned to search for his lost childhood through the children of others. Is he at times Captain Hook, capturing innocent babes with his iron hand and crooked smile? The crocodile is always close, ticking away with a clock inside, just as death is ever-present in reality but denied in the fantasy of Neverland where no one ever grows up, and all inhabitants move unceasingly in the same direction.

This psychoanalytic book is a profound meditation on the use of stories to explore the hidden phantasy structures as metaphors for understanding the psychological processes of growing up. It also illustrates how traumatic this process of maturation can be when impacted by tragedies not only personal but historical. Wars, plagues, and natural disasters have had enormous influence on the individual and social psyche and its evolution through time. What will be the effects of COVID-19 on a generation of children today, given its isolation and destructiveness throughout families and society, together with the existential threats of global warming?

The original book, *Peter Pan ou l'enfant triste*, was published in France by Calmann-Lévy in 1992. A second edition came out in 2005 with continuous sales today. Kathleen Kelley-Lainé has written a tour de force and its publication in English by Phoenix is to be congratulated.

# CHAPTER 1

# Peter Pan is born

'Mummy, did you know how to fly when you were little?' The question seemed to come out of the blue, but my son's face was earnest. When I was a child I had my own vital questions: 'If I wasn't I, who would I be?' 'If I wasn't here, where would I be?' I answered him, 'Yes, my darling, I did know how to fly.' Perhaps circumstances forced me to learn and never to forget the art of flying, of soaring over life's tragedies until they became so small as to disappear from sight. I dreamt of 'Once upon a time, was there ever a time, perhaps there was never a time'. All Hungarian fairy tales open with these magic words.

Like Peter Pan, who flew out the window shortly after his birth to avoid growing up, I made 'nowhere' my home, and 'Neverland' my universe. I suppose that I met Peter Pan rather early in life, maybe on the day I was born when my father first held me in his arms and ordained me with his most intimate wishes: 'Here is Doctor Kanitz Katalin!'

Words pronounced upon the heads of newborn babes are always heavy with meaning; they can sometimes be so important as to determine the entire life of a person. Was it the word 'doctor' that frightened me enough to make me fly away to Kensington Gardens, just like baby Peter Pan? Or more likely the weight of my father's dreams behind those famous words must have borne heavily upon my cradle. Nevertheless, I didn't move. After all, I had just arrived, a tired little thing having survived the adventure of birth, and the warmth of his hands felt good; those hands that were to become so very important for me. Peter, on the other hand, was absolutely convinced that babies are birds before they are born, and that he could still remember how to fly, which is why he decided to slip out of the window without any hesitation …

## Like a bird

Well, Peter Pan climbed onto the window-sill from where he could see the tops of the trees, certainly those of Kensington Gardens. He immediately forgot that he was a little boy in a nightdress, and away he flew, right over the houses to the Gardens. It was extraordinary that he could fly without wings, even though he felt a terrible itch between his shoulders where normally wings were placed. Who knows, perhaps we all could fly if we were as convinced as Peter Pan was that evening. The advantage of such power is that it offers the possibility of travelling through time; grown-ups, however, don't dare take the risk of soaring around like Peter Pan for fear of falling backwards, into Neverland.

Peter landed so successfully in the Gardens that his first reaction was to lie on his back and wriggle his legs in the air. He had already forgotten that he was a human being and honestly thought he was a bird. He could have answered my first question immediately: 'If I wasn't me, who would I be?' 'A bird!'

The assurance of one's ability to fly is often accompanied by a certain lightness of being that facilitates all sorts of dislocations. In principle, when a baby is firmly held in its mother's arms, a comforting sensation of gravity installs itself together with the reassuring impression of becoming a 'me'. Gradually the wings fall off; the baby gains weight and sufficient confidence to start its journey in time without wanting to constantly look back. This conviction of 'being' is accompanied by the capacity to feel and to love.

In fact, one wonders whether Peter Pan felt anything at all upon his arrival in the Gardens. For example, he had to watch the fairies carry their pails to milk the cows before he realised that he was thirsty. He therefore flew over to the Round Pond with the intention of plunging in his beak, but of course it was only his nose! He did succeed, however, in sipping a little bit of water, but it was not as refreshing as usual. Then he tried a puddle, and fell right into it.

When a real bird falls into water, he spreads out his feathers and pecks them dry, but Peter could not remember what to do and decided rather sulkily to go to sleep on the weeping-beech in the Baby Walk where sad children go to have a good cry.

A little later terrible noises woke him, but as is often the case with very 'light' individuals he was unable to locate where the sounds were coming from. Were they inside or outside his body? In reality he ignored the fact that the terrible noises were his very own sneezes.

He desired something so very much, he knew he wanted it with all his might, but he could not figure out what it was. What he really wanted was for his mother to blow his nose, but since he ignored that fact he decided to consult the fairies.

Babies, not having acquired significant weight in their mother's arms, or for whom the sensation of 'being' was interrupted by a tragic event, risk becoming lost children condemned to fly around in Time searching for a piece of their lost childhood.

It is often the case that a lost child, in the effort not to cry over his or her lost childhood, will lose the capacity to feel; from then on, there is no telling what comes from inside or outside. Like Peter Pan in Kensington Gardens, he is obliged to ask someone, for example, a fairy, to tell him what is happening.

I once met a little boy who was terribly sad at having lost his childhood, even though no one suspected he was lost, or that he had lost his childhood. He never stopped drawing aeroplanes, always the same ones. On one occasion, despite shaking his head with energetic 'no's, we were able to evoke his sadness, and I even detected a small tear in the corner of his eye. With few words he told me how unhappy he had been when his parents obliged him to leave the house where he was born. He was still wearing nappies, and his mother already had a new baby in her tummy.

He certainly did not want to know how babies are made, so we never raised the issue again. Nevertheless, from the day of the tiny tear his drawings changed: he began elaborating long sinuous underground tunnels wherein very complicated, terrible, and mysterious conflicts occurred. I knew from then on that he had landed a little. In leaving the sky, he was able to imagine contacting the feelings inside, while discovering that they would not kill him.

## The nightgown

Peter Pan wanted to escape the destiny of a human being so much that he decided to remain a bird just as he was before his birth. Alas, it was not enough simply to have landed in Kensington Gardens; one also had to be accepted by its inhabitants, the fairies. In fact the fairies were afraid of Peter Pan. He seemed so strange in his little white nightgown that as soon as they saw him they fled to all corners of the Gardens.

Seeing the fairies running away in all directions when he tried to speak to them, Peter had to admit at last that there was a problem. He therefore decided to consult the wisest bird in the Gardens, Solomon Caw, to tell him about his difficulties. Solomon Caw was of invaluable support to Peter Pan as he was able to help him understand that in fact he was not a 'bird' but a little 'human being in a white nightgown'.

'Look at your nightgown if you don't believe me,' Solomon said; and with staring eyes Peter looked at his nightgown, and then at the sleeping birds. Not one of them wore anything.

'Ruffle your feathers,' said that grim old Solomon, and Peter tried most desperately hard to ruffle his feathers, but he had none. Then he rose up, quaking, and for the first time since he stood on the window-ledge, he remembered a lady who had been very fond of him.

'I think I shall go back to Mother,' he murmured timidly.

'Goodbye,' replied Solomon Caw with a queer look.

But Peter hesitated. 'Why don't you go?' the old one asked politely.

'I suppose,' said Peter huskily, 'I suppose I can still fly?'

You see he had lost faith.

'Poor little half-and-half!' said Solomon, who was not really hard-hearted. 'You will never be able to fly again, not even on windy days. You must live here on the Serpentine island always.'

'And never even go to the Kensington Gardens?' Peter asked tragically.

'How could you get across?' said Solomon. He promised very kindly, however, to teach Peter as many of the bird ways as could be learned by one of such an awkward shape.

'Then I shan't be exactly a human?' Peter asked.

'No.'

'Nor exactly a bird?'

'No.'

'What shall I be?'

'You will be a Betwixt-and-Between,' Solomon said, and certainly he was a wise old fellow, for that is exactly how it turned out.

It is sometimes vital to consult someone in order to discover the feelings of a 'human being'.

But the best thing Solomon had done was to teach him to have a joyful heart under all circumstances. All birds have joyful hearts unless you rob their nests. It was the only kind of heart that Solomon knew, so it was easy for him to teach Peter how to get one.

Peter's heart became so joyful that he felt he must sing just as the birds sing for joy all day long. The fact that he was partly human posed a problem, for unlike birds he needed an instrument. He therefore improvised a flute out of reeds, and in the evening he would sit on the shore practising to imitate the sighs of the wind and the ripple of the water.

At other times, as Peter sat by the shore tootling divinely on his pipe, sad thoughts arose, and his music became sad. The reason for all this sadness was the impossibility of reaching the Gardens, although he could see them through the arch of the bridge. He knew he could never be a real human again, and scarcely wanted to be one, but oh how he longed to play as other children play, and of course there is no such lovely place to play in as the Gardens.

## The first wish

The proof that he remained a boy despite everything was the mighty desire to see his mother. He managed to find a way by tricking the fairies; he asked them to grant him his dearest desire, to be able to fly once more to return to his mother. The Queen of the Fairies tried to dissuade him:

> 'Will the window be open?'
>
> 'Of course!' replied Peter, absolutely sure of himself. 'Mother always keeps it open in the hope that I may fly back.'
>
> 'How do you know?' they asked, quite surprised, and really Peter could not explain how he knew.
>
> 'I just know,' he said.

The window was wide open, just as he knew it would be, and in he fluttered. There was his mother lying asleep. Peter alighted softly on the wooden rail at the foot of the bed and had a good look at her. She lay with her head on her hand, and the hollow in the pillow was like a nest lined with her brown wavy hair. He remembered, though he had long forgotten it, that she always gave her hair a holiday at night. How sweet the frills of her nightgown were! He was very glad she was such a pretty mother.

But she looked sad, and he sensed why she looked sad. One of her arms moved as if it wanted to go around something, and he knew what it wanted to go around.

> 'O Mother,' said Peter to himself. 'If only you knew who is sitting on the rail at the foot of the bed.'

Very gently he patted the little mound that her feet made, and he could see by her face that she liked it. He knew he had but to say 'Mother' ever so softly, and she would wake up. They always wake up at once if it is you that says their name. Then she would give such a joyous cry and squeeze him tight. How nice that would be to him, but oh! how exquisitely delicious it would be to her. That, I am afraid, is how Peter regarded it. In returning to his mother he never doubted that he was giving her the greatest treat a woman can have. Nothing can be more splendid, he thought, than to have a little boy of your own. How proud of him they are! And very rightly so.

But why does Peter sit so long on the rail; why does he not tell his mother that he has come back?

I quite shrink from the truth, which is that he sat there in two minds. Sometimes he looked longingly at his mother, and sometimes he looked longingly at the window. Certainly, it would be pleasant to be her boy again, but on the other hand, what times those had been in the Gardens! Was he so sure that he should enjoy wearing clothes again? He popped off the bed and opened some drawers to have a look at his old garments. They were still there, but he could not remember how to put them on. The socks, for instance, were they worn on the hands or on the feet? He was about to try one of them on his hand, when he had a great adventure. Perhaps the drawer had creaked; at any rate, his mother woke up, for he heard her say 'Peter', as if it was the loveliest word in the language. He remained sitting on the floor and held his breath, wondering how she knew that he had come back. If she said 'Peter', again, he meant to cry 'Mother' and run to her. But she spoke no more, she made little moans only, and when he next peeped at her she was once more asleep, with tears on her cheeks.

It made Peter very miserable, and what do you think was the first thing he did? Sitting on the rail at the foot of the bed, he played a beautiful lullaby to his mother on his pipe. He had composed it himself from the way she said 'Peter', and he never stopped playing until she looked happy.

While playing his instrument he thought himself so clever that he could scarcely resist wakening her to hear her say, 'O Peter, how exquisitely you play!' However, as she now seemed comfortable, he again cast looks at the window. You must not think that he wanted to fly away and never come back. He had quite decided to be his mother's boy, but hesitated about beginning that very night …

## The promise to return

Once one has lost the sweet feeling of gravity in mother's arms, it is difficult, perhaps impossible, to find it again. But the memory of it persists, and one often tries to feign the sensation even if one doesn't feel it, just like Peter Pan.

Twice he came back from the window, intending to kiss his mother, but decided against it for fear of waking her, so he chose to play a marvellous kiss on his flute before flying back to the Gardens for good.

Many nights and even months passed by before Peter asked the fairies to allow him to fly back again: first of all he wanted to say his goodbyes not only to his friends but also to his favourite places. Then he took his last sail in the boat, then his very last sail in the boat, then his truly last sail in the boat …

There was no real urgency, he thought, as his mother would never weary of waiting for him. So when at last he said to them bravely, 'I wish now to go back to mother for ever and always,' they had to tickle his shoulders and let him go.

He went in a hurry in the end, because he had dreamt that his mother was crying, and he knew he was the great thing she cried for, and that a hug from her splendid Peter would quickly make her smile. Oh! He felt sure of it, and so eager was he to be nestling in her arms that this time he flew straight to the window, which was always open for him. But the window was closed, with iron bars, and peering inside he saw his mother sleeping peacefully with her arm around another little boy.

Peter cried out, 'Mother! Mother!' but she heard him not; in vain, he beat his little fists against the iron bars. He had to fly back, sobbing, to the Gardens and he never saw his darling mother again. What a glorious boy he had meant to be to her! Ah, Peter! We who have made the great mistake, how different we would be with a second chance. But Solomon was right—there is no second chance for most of us. When we reach the window, it is closing time. The iron bars are up for life.

## Parents' dreams

My mother's dreams began well before I was conceived. She already had a boy so she imagined a little girl, blonde with blue eyes, who could dance. I was blonde with blue eyes and loved to dance. My weight was already established before arrival; it was only later that I acquired the lightness of Peter Pan.

Without a doubt, my father was firmly held in his mother's arms. He thus gained sufficient weight to anchor his sense of 'being': he was the first son, and he was charming!

However, I suspect that he met Peter Pan rather early in life; otherwise, how could he have used the strategy of 'flight' so often?

The first time must have been when he discovered a little brother who had taken his spot in the cradle. Had he wanted to keep his mother to himself forever?

This original wound never quite healed, and opened up again at the birth of his son. It was so painful that he was unable to set eyes on the little intruder right away. It was therefore much easier, later on, to plant all his dreams in a daughter.

My mother encountered Peter Pan in a different way. As the last daughter of a family of thirteen children she probably weighed less heavily in her mother's dreams. In fact, she stole the place of her little sister, who was not ready to give up her status as 'the baby'. She was such a merry and charming child but became overwhelmed with sadness at the birth of my mother. She even stopped laughing and singing. As a result my grandmother felt guilty and found it difficult to take care of her newborn baby under the jealous gaze of the little sister. The family legend told of how little Ida cried persistently, day and night, in a desperate effort to attract the vital presence of her mother!

Peter Pan is often present around the question of life and death. He waits for the right moment to whisk up a child who may have fallen from his perambulator, not having been held sufficiently. This type of accident, often due to parental neglect, can also be the result of too much love, and curiously enough the effect is the same.

At age two my mother came down with diphtheria. Her older sister left her sitting for hours in a cold and humid corner of the cellar. The next day she was choking to death. Her face was already black when my grandmother, in a moment of drastic lucidity, took a wooden spoon, reached down her throat and succeeded in getting rid of some of the thick matter blocking the air passage. My mother survived, but forgot her baby words and her first steps and had to be taught how to walk and talk all over again. I often heard her say musingly, 'What if she had let me die?'

Both my parents encountered Peter Pan early in life. But it was perhaps my grandmother who came into closest contact with him. She had a little sister whose sole passion was to play 'burials'. She buried everything—her dolls, dead birds, flies, and chicken bones. She was a pale, transparent-looking creature, and the contrast with my robust, rosy-cheeked little grandmother was almost scandalous. Little Emiko, despite her morose character, and eternal 'No, I don't want any' was her mother's favourite when it came to eating. She died on her fourth birthday and no one knew why. During the burial ceremony my grandmother kept close behind her mother—was it to make sure not to lose her? Nevertheless, she was near enough to catch those terrible words that remain engraved forever: 'Why didn't Elizabeth die instead?'

A mother who wishes a death, a mother who saves a life, is a mother the child cannot leave. It is as if her arms were not safe: she either holds the child too tightly, or she is ready to drop it. The child is not free to acquire the feeling of just 'being', and the dream of a soft mother with whom it is so good to 'be' remains the child's quest for a lifetime.

Even if he perches on the window-sill and tries to fly off, the child will not be able to tear himself away from the fatal attraction of 'Mother', guardian of the tantalising secret of life and death.

I have met people who remain on life's window-sill forever, incapable of making a choice. They don't dare to turn back for fear of meeting the terrible 'she', nor can they live without her proximity. They feel addicted to her substance, like a drug.

Peter Pan found a clever solution by going to live in Neverland: that cosy little island probably reminded him of his mother's arms even though the length of his journey gave him the impression of having left her.

There are various methods for giving oneself the illusion of having left the 'Goddess Mother' while keeping her firmly implanted in one's soul. The strategy of 'flight' can take on a number of different forms, but Peter Pan's departures are readily discernible by their ephemeral nature, as well as by his cocky laughter mocking us from the top of a cloud, or simply from the corner of the street.

One of the most important characteristics of these flights is the nostalgic desire to be held in mother's arms, and to relive those strong baby sensations they shared at the very beginning. All these departures are in fact desperate attempts at finding a second chance, especially when the feeling of 'being human' has not been established with sufficient force. Such flights are looked upon as great adventures, while in fact the eternal search for lost childhood is a real tragedy.

## The hour of departure

We were convinced of experiencing one of the greatest adventures the night all four of us flew out the window in search of a foreign land where there would be no more tragedies and where we would live happily ever after. We left our home one wintry night while all the neighbours were still asleep … our home that was later to become the Neverland of my life.

Why such a sudden departure? I didn't dare to ask that question until now. At the time it all seemed very clear and later it became a story that we persisted in telling ourselves to justify events. With passing years it turned into a souvenir that I would pull out of a drawer whenever someone asked me, 'In fact, where do you come from?' My father was Jewish. When the Germans arrived in Hungary, Jews were collected and taken to camps and disappeared. Many were simply shot and thrown into the Danube.

My mother was horrified as she witnessed the long lines of victims being forced towards the river: it was winter, the water was frozen, so they made holes in the ice … 'No! No! Please sir, I am too young; I want to live!' The young adolescent's red hair flashed like blood against the grey sky. My mother closed the window, but was never able to eradicate the image.

On the day the superintendent received orders to gather all the Jews in our building, my father was coerced into joining the line-up on the sidewalk. Women and children and old people were sent to houses with a yellow star and the men to labour camps. It was Christmas. I was two years old. The living room looked especially desolate, as there was no tree.

I remember my mother sitting on a chair in the middle of the room, crying. In her lap was a crumpled piece of paper indicating the labour camp where my father had been deported. In a few weeks he would be shipped off to Germany. The bombs crashed over Budapest, and people rushed to their basements. My brother put me into a basket and started to run; I must have been very light indeed. The sirens, the planes, and the bombs exploding both frightened and fascinated me. The damp cold of the cellar wall penetrated my back as I leaned against it, singing as loudly as I could. Some people smiled at the charming child. Was I trying to cheer up the sad faces? Nothing could ever happen to me; this was a great adventure!

One day my brother and I remained alone, running from the flat to the basement; we couldn't find Mother. She was too anxious and scrupulous not to have told us where she was going! 'Your parents are dead; your parents are dead,' a little neighbour kept repeating with a kind of joy I never understood.

My mother had received a message informing her that my father was free. He succeeded in escaping from the camp. The guards had herded the prisoners toward the trains destined for Germany. They were shuffling slowly in a long line when my father noticed the open basement window of a factory. He jumped in without being noticed. The workers chased him out immediately, but the line of prisoners had passed and my father was not missed. He was able to reach Budapest and notify my mother. A hiding place had to be found immediately; there was no question of coming home. My mother was desperate to find a safe place. The family printing firm was the first obvious choice; surely his secretary would have a good solution! But it was already closing time, and the office was locked; this was fortunate as it turned out later that the secretary was a militant Nazi.

She found him waiting for her in the shadow of a doorway in Vaci Utca. Was it really he? So thin and haggard with borrowed clothes sagging on his back; he who was always so elegant and well-groomed … only his smile had not changed, but there was no time for long embraces; they had to hurry … Where to go? Where to hide? 'To your brother, of course … no one will suspect anything …'

My father spent the rest of the war crouched in a cupboard at his brother-in-law's apartment. Feri knew he risked both his life and that of his family, but he was a very good-hearted man. The day my father was blown out of his hiding place by the pressure of a bomb dropped nearby, he was obliged to go down to the basement with everyone else.

'Here is my cousin who has just come up from the country.' That was how my uncle Feri introduced his brother-in-law to the neighbours. He was a tall, well-respected, handsome man, and no one questioned his word. My father survived when he was meant to perish.

## Apu comes home

Father's return home is still vividly engraved in my memory. It must have been around midday as my mother was preparing lunch on the makeshift open fire that served as our wartime kitchen in the courtyard of our building. Other women were also busy preparing food, and I spent my time wandering back and forth between the yard and the street. On one of my trips my eye caught the form of a man walking toward me on the pavement. His steps seemed strangely familiar and suddenly, without knowing why, I found myself running into his open arms …

Who was this man? Where had he gone? Why did he come back? Had they lied to me? 'Daddy has left on a trip. Daddy is in the country. Daddy will be back soon.' 'Daddy, Daddy, Apu, Apu!'

From then on, life seemingly returned to normal, until the day when it was the Russians who hounded my father. They needed a certain number of Hungarian prisoners to take back to Russia. After all, this country had sided with the Germans. They rounded up people all over the city, sometimes forcing entry to individuals' apartments in the middle of the night for unknown motives. They used the same methods as the Germans, only this time the reasons were that of 'class' and not of 'race'. But we were targeted once again. Despite the apparent normality of everyday life, my father was increasingly anxious about the menace of 'history'.

It became clear that we had to leave, run, escape, and fly away. My father was experienced, only this time he had his family with him. Surprisingly, Christmas was remarkable! Santa Claus, exceptionally generous, brought me: a beautiful doll, a crib, books, and a magnificent pen for my first written words. A gloriously decorated tree reached the ceiling of our apartment. Granny had made more beiglis than usual, those delicious traditional Hungarian nut and poppy-seed cakes I adored. My mother wore a silk dress and smelled of the sweet French perfume her husband had bought for her in Paris. My father seemed strangely absent; was it worry that stole his smile?

A few days later, he announced that we were leaving on a winter holiday. It was as unexpected and brutal as the day he revealed that we had changed our name. This event occurred, I must admit, following an incident in my school. The teacher called me 'that Kanitz girl' with so much hate in her voice that I asked my father why we had such an ugly name. Two days later our name was 'Christianised' to Kellei. My mother was not happy about the changed name. Yes, the war was over, and some Jewish families had changed their name in an attempt to escape the Nazis' final solution, but why do it in 1948, after all we had survived?

## Travelling without baggage

Before leaving, my father told us we could not take much baggage; no dolls, no crib, no books, even my new pen remained on the table. I had to be very light on this vacation; I chose to take my little stuffed rabbit. Years later I understood that the little rabbit symbolised a moment of great joy in my childhood. I remember being woken by my smiling parents on the day I turned five; they were holding a gift—it was the little rabbit. I felt enveloped by their love, the warmth of their presence. I was happy and I knew it!

The suitcases were finally ready. As my father locked the door, I ran down the stairs full of joy and expectation. To my surprise a large black automobile was waiting for us in the street. We didn't drive in cars much in those days, and it seemed very odd that we should be afforded this luxury. It was night, but the stars were not shining as brightly as on the Christmas eve when my brother took me out for a walk in the snow while our parents decorated the tree … I took a last glance at our windows, and imagined letting my fingers run around the wrought-iron trimming of the balcony. The same feeling returned many years later when I saw our house again.

I hugged my little rabbit very tightly and felt sad about abandoning my new doll even if it was only for a short vacation.

Before leaving Budapest, we stopped at the home of some strange people I didn't know. I was astonished by their sombre appearance; a woman dressed in black spoke to my mother about things that I couldn't understand. We had to leave our suitcases at their place.

'Of course we will send you all your valuable objects … of course.'

'Come here, little one, give me your rabbit; my son will keep it for you.'

The woman in black smiled at me knowingly. My mother did not hear my silent cry for help. I needed her protection, I wanted her to save my rabbit, I wanted her to put out her arms to prevent the tragedy … but she was absent, her look was empty. For the first time in my life I felt completely alone, and helpless. I had to relinquish my little rabbit.

Our next stop was in the country, in the basement of someone's house. A group of men in uniforms were huddled together on the cold floor while we waited for others to arrive. My father warned me not to speak. 'We must be very quiet not to wake the people sleeping upstairs.' Then he whispered in my ear: 'They don't know we are here; it's a secret!' What an adventure!

A little later we were instructed to split into two groups. It was agreed that my father and brother would continue by bicycle; my mother and I, disguised in scarves to look like peasants from the country, were to take a bus with another woman. If anyone should ask me the question, I was to say that the lady was my mother and my mother was my aunt. I didn't understand a thing and yet somehow I understood it all. Images of the countryside rushed by the windows of the bus, and the wheels sang 'goodbye, goodbye, goodbye …' until we finally arrived at a large farm. There were a thousand things for a city child like myself to discover, but I was told not to play: 'Stay close to the house, and if you see a mounted policeman come in immediately. Take the gold chain off your neck; it could attract attention.'

I was chasing the geese and ducks when two men in uniform stopped me short. My heart began pounding violently, and I ran to find my mother; she turned as white as a sheet. 'Your papers, please!' My mother fainted and the two men burst into laughter: 'Mrs, you mustn't take things so hard. We have come to help you. It was just a joke, that's all!' The two jokers were our 'passers', come to take us over the border to Austria. It took some time to reassure my mother; she was never able to laugh about it.

We crossed the border, ostensibly more of a gutter than a significant political barrier. The electric fencing that later represented the 'iron curtain' had not yet been installed, and all that was needed was a little jump to get to the other side. I thought it was great fun to ride on the shoulders of one of the jokers in uniform who helped us across. Once in Austria, we walked for a long time through fields and forests before reaching our destination, the farmhouse where we would spend the night. All was silent, but I seemed to hear my father whisper, 'We are free!' Bowls of warm milk awaited us; the simple, comforting welcome of the farm family felt like a blessing. We all slept in the same large room with the grandfather, his little grandson, and the Christmas tree that was still in place. I shared a bed with my mother, and despite the reassuring warmth of her body, I had great difficulty in falling asleep. The next morning she revealed that we had left Hungary forever. At last I was able to cry: 'Oh, my doll! My little rabbit, I have lost you; I shall never, never find you again!'

# CHAPTER 2

# Peter Pan on the window-sill

The freedom to come and go, to know that Mother's eyes are on her little one, waiting, gazing beyond the open window … these are some of the necessary conditions for a child to experience his childhood with love and be willing to let it go one day to grow up.

Peter wanted to leave just for a short while to play with the fairies, but he also longed to see his mother again, to make sure that she was waiting for him and that he continued to exist in her heart. Confronted with the window barred, a new baby in his cradle, everything familiar had disappeared. Peter no longer had a mother or a cradle; he experienced the greatest tragedy that could ever happen to a child. He cried desperately at the closed bars, thumping his little fists on the window pane … he had lost his childhood.

When the border closed behind us, my parents knew that there was no turning back. I cried over the dolls abandoned in our home, those rooms that would be deprived of our laughter, but did I know that it was my childhood that I was leaving behind at No. 20 Mar Jenö Utca?

Even if we do not recognise the weight of such tragedies immediately, each one of us has an ancient persisting reminiscence that we ignore. Peter was dreadfully sad in front of the closed window. The soreness he felt in his arms and legs reminded him vaguely of an ancient discomfort of long ago. Was it the memory of a bird? Was it the recollection of a baby? Or was it something in between? Did he suddenly sense the gravity of the agony that he had once felt when leaving the original nest? It is very difficult for a human being to grow up, as it requires abandoning a nest where one was ever so comfortable.

I once watched a mother squirrel teach her young to leave the nest and spring from tree to tree. She used a mother's trick: she rubbed her teats close to the little one's nose, pretending she would suckle him, and then she jumped onto the next branch. The little squirrel trembled with fear, but the desire for his mother's warm milk finally gave him the necessary courage to jump higher and higher up the tree.

## A moment's distraction

Leaving and returning allows us to revisit our old nest from time to time, and reassures us about who we were until this becomes unnecessary, because who we were in the past has become an integral part of who we are now.

A mother's initial task is to learn how to trick her little one so that he/she does not regret having left the original nest, that is, the mother's tummy. Generally mothers are immediately prepared for this task and are very adept at giving cuddles and looks that make babies forget that they were birds. We may suspect that Peter's mother could not fool him, and that is why he flew out the window so quickly. On the other hand, he didn't really give her much time. Some mothers need time: for even if they have been expecting the little bird with passion, when he finally does arrive, they are unable to do what it takes to make him not regret leaving the nest.

It is also the moment when mothers tend to dream about the time when they were little birds. They can even forget their own tiny one who is waiting. Perhaps it was during one of these moments of his mother's inattention that Peter flew out of the window for the first time. Later, when he told the story to Wendy, he said it was because his mother had forgotten to weigh him. It certainly is true that one must weigh babies as soon as they arrive to guarantee the solidness that keeps them from flying off.

The question of weight is both essential and vital. When a child has had to live through heavy tragedies too early on in life, rather than weighing in his own body, the weight presses so heavily on his past that he is obliged to fly off to escape from being crushed. If the weight is a tomb, it is even more difficult to carry.

You can recognise a lost child by his uncommon lightness of being in either his physical appearance or mental state of mind. Clowns are among the saddest persons on earth.

When the window is barred, and when borders are wired with electric fencing, there is no turning back; the past takes on heaviness, a kind of gravity that dissolves without one knowing it into the lost paradise of childhood origins. The child, in an attempt to gain weight-lessness, lets go of many attributes, including having to choose his/her sexuality.

Being a girl or boy is a greater responsibility for a lost child than being both at once or nothing at all. Choosing one's gender means accepting to grow up and of dying one day. Angels, for example, are asexual; but they have wings instead. Flying becomes all-powerful!

## The adventure of growing up

Peter had to abandon coming home to his mother again; desperately wounded, he returned to Kensington Gardens and decided never ever to pronounce the word 'Mother'.

Suddenly the Gardens lost all their appeal; he forgot how to play, and even the fairies were unable to cheer him up. Only Tinker Bell, the most amusing of all the fairies, succeeded in raising his interest a little. She told him wonderful stories about Neverland, and that is how he decided to go and live there and have endless adventures with the pirates and Indians and the 'lost boys' who had fallen out of their prams when the nurse was not looking. He decided to become their leader. The adventures of Peter Pan begin as follows:

> All children grow up, except one. They soon know that they will grow up, and the way Wendy knew was this. One day when she was two years old she was playing in a garden, and she plucked another flower and ran with it to her mother. I suppose she must have looked rather delightful, for Mrs Darling put her hand to her heart and cried, 'Oh, why can't you remain like this forever!' This was all that

passed between them on the subject, but henceforth Wendy knew that she must grow up. You always know after you are two. Two is the beginning of the end.

The story of Peter Pan is the story of a lost child, a child so lost that he refuses to grow up. Usually stories pave the way; Peter Pan's story demonstrates how to stand still forever, in Neverland.

## The Darling family's window

Despite all the fascinating adventures he had in Neverland, Peter Pan still felt the need to journey to London from time to time. Sensing a nostalgic yearning among the lost boys for stories and fairy tales, Peter decided to fly regularly to London and sit on the window-sill of a real family and listen to a real mother telling stories to real children. This is how he landed one evening at the Darling family at No. 14: Mr and Mrs Darling and their three children, Wendy, the eldest daughter, and the two boys, Michael and John.

When you come to know Peter Pan, you can imagine that he didn't land on that particular window by chance. Even if the Darling family seems to be just an ordinary English family at first sight, there must have been a little crack that Peter slid into; otherwise, how could he have become so important to them. Let us begin with Mrs Darling.

She was a beautiful lady with a romantic mind and a sweet mocking mouth. Her romantic mind was like those tiny boxes of varying sizes, one inside the other, that come from the mysterious East. When you have managed to open one, you discover there is still another inside.

Mrs Darling was one of those women whom you cannot know completely. Was Peter Pan hiding in one of the boxes? In any case the kiss that was on the right-hand corner of her sweet mocking mouth, the one that her daughter Wendy could never obtain, was certainly for him!

Mrs Darling first heard of Peter when she was tidying up her children's minds. It is the nightly custom of every good mother after her children are asleep to rummage in their minds and put things straight for the next morning, repacking into their proper places the many articles that had wandered during the day.

On her knees she lingers humorously over some of the contents, wondering where her children had picked this up, making discoveries sweet and not so sweet, pressing this to her cheek as if it were as nice as a kitten, and hurriedly stowing it out of sight. When her children wake in the morning, the naughtiness and evil passions with which they went to bed have been folded up small and placed at the bottom of their minds; on the top, beautifully aired, are spread the prettier thoughts ready to be put on the next day.

## Mothers' wishes

I know that all mothers tend to rummage around in their children's heads, but Mrs Darling was so intent on putting her little ones' thoughts in order that one may suspect she feared they would escape her. After all, she had so wanted to have children, even against her husband's wishes!

It is customary for mothers to create their babies in collaboration with their husbands. Even so, they may begin by drawing babies on their own, leaving nothing to chance … thereby mastering all their features: the nose, the mouth, the eyes. They often have someone in mind, resembling a sister, a brother, a grandfather: it may be in the hope of keeping the child forever. We saw Mrs Darling in the garden with her little two-year-old daughter: the child was so deliciously beautiful as she ran towards her mother to offer her a flower that she pronounced these terrible words: 'Oh, if you could only stay like this forever!'

Such maternal nostalgia 'if only' can have very contradictory effects on a child: sometimes it is precisely those words that make the child understand (as did Wendy) that one must grow up. At other times it works, and the child does not grow.

It can happen that a lost child may unconsciously feel that he or she must not grow beyond a certain age. I knew a young mother who had lost a child of three in an accident. Many years later she gave birth to another boy who resembled the dead child so much that she had the impression the dead one had come back! The second boy became a lost child at three; he had reached the age of his dead brother, his growth stopped developing. Did he fear he would lose his mother's love?

Mothers who don't want their children to grow up tend to hang on to their 'status' as mother. Being a mother is one way of finding one's own mother: the one that is lost, the one that one never had, the kind of mother that one would have liked to have. The little girl inside Mrs Darling was probably still very close to her feelings, ready to pop out at any time, wanting to make them heard. Finding Peter Pan again was her way of recovering her lost childhood. But she was to pay the price of that encounter.

As she was constantly looking for the little lost boy, she often bumped into him in the thoughts of her children. The word Peter was coming back and she couldn't understand why; she knew no one by that name. When remembering her own childhood it all came back. They used to tell strange stories about him, for example, when a child died, he accompanied him for part of the way so that he wouldn't be afraid. At the time she believed he really existed, but now that she was married and full of good sense, she had serious doubts.

> 'Furthermore,' she said to Wendy, 'he must have grown up by now.'
> 'Oh no, he hasn't grown up,' assured Wendy with great conviction, 'he is exactly my size.'

Mrs Darling consulted Mr Darling, but he just smiled ironically:

> 'It is surely those silly things that Nana puts into their heads; that's what you get for having a dog for a nurse; it is just like the sort of idea that she would have! Stop talking to them about it, and it will go away.'

But 'it' didn't go away, and soon that troublesome boy came to cause Mrs Darling a real shock.

## The power of a dream

Children are capable of having the strangest adventures without batting an eyelid. For example, they can tell you a story about their father one week after his death: that they met him in the forest, having set him a trap and it was such great fun! At that moment death is no problem for them; it has no weight.

An attentive mother knows how to make up for such lightness of being in her children. Mrs Darling, however, was still dreaming about 'once upon a time'.

While she was asleep, she visualised Neverland drawing near and a strange boy breaking through it. He did not alarm her, for she had seen him on the faces of many childless women. Perhaps he is to be found behind the faces of some mothers as well. But in her dream he tore the screen that obscures Neverland, and she saw Wendy and John and Michael peeping through the gap.

The image by itself would have been trivial, but while she was dreaming the window of the nursery was blown open by a gust of wind and a boy did drop onto the floor. He was accompanied by a strange light, no bigger than your fist, which darted about the room like a living thing; it was without a doubt this light that wakened Mrs Darling.

She started up with a cry, and saw the boy, and somehow she knew at once that he was Peter Pan. He was a lovely boy, clad in skeleton leaves and the juices that ooze out of trees, but the most entrancing thing about him was that he had all his baby teeth. When he saw she was a grown-up, he gnashed the little pearls at her. Mrs Darling screamed and, as if in answer to a bell, the door opened, and Nana entered, returned from her evening out. She growled and sprang at the boy, who leapt lightly through the window. Again Mrs Darling screamed, this time in distress for him, for she thought he was killed, and she ran down into the street to look for his little body, but it was not there; and she looked up, and in the black night she could see nothing but what she thought was a shooting star …

Upon her return to the nursery, she found Nana with something in her mouth, which proved to be the boy's shadow. As he leapt at the window Nana had closed it quickly, too late to catch him, but his shadow had not had time to get out; slam went the window and snapped it off.

Mrs Darling examined the shadow carefully; it was quite the ordinary kind. She thought of showing it to Mr Darling, but he was doing his calculations for winter coats for John and Michael, with a wet towel around his head to keep his brain clear, and it seemed a shame to trouble him. She therefore decided to fold up the shadow and put it carefully in the top drawer of the dresser, until she could find the opportune moment to speak of it to Mr Darling.

## A father's role

Had Mr Darling, the father, been able to protect his family, Mrs Darling's lost childhood would not have been enough to encourage Peter Pan to sneak in the window of No. 14. However, it was not the case. His wife had made several attempts to warn him of the danger of this strange person, but Mr Darling was too fragile himself, with very low self-esteem, which meant that he was particularly vulnerable to Peter Pan's 'incursions'.

A father often finds it difficult to maintain a suitable role between his mother, his wife, and his children, especially when he has not had sufficient support from his own father. A wife can either facilitate the father's role in relation to his children or make it very difficult. We noticed that Mrs Darling preferred to draw her children's faces alone, without her husband. Perhaps it was also because Mr Darling was constantly delving into his accounts that he didn't take the time to participate in sketching his children.

One must know of course that fathers' reasons for counting so ardently is to relieve the anxiety of losing their place when the child arrives. It is particularly true for the first one, and once there are several the battle for the centre of attention becomes a habit. Some fathers abandon their families under such circumstances and try to find a central place elsewhere. Others don't leave but never get used to it and just end up counting.

Mr Darling was particularly sensitive to what the neighbours thought; he hoped that their esteem would make him feel better about himself. It was because of the neighbours that he felt ashamed of having a dog for a nurse, even though he knew that no nursery could be better kept. After all, he had his place in the city to think of! Furthermore, Nana troubled him in other ways: he sometimes felt that she didn't admire him. 'I know she admires you tremendously, George,' Mrs Darling would assure him, and then she would sign to the children to be especially nice to father.

The most bothersome of all was Mr Darling's behaviour. Although he was the most discreet and anonymous person outside the home, with his family he just let go, and blew hot and cold without hesitation.

It is often the case that the father of a sad child resembles Mr Darling. Many men have told me how much they had longed for a father capable of protecting their childhood, and the profound deception they felt when they realised that their father was just another child.

Sometimes a child in this situation hangs on to the image of his grandfather. This is what the little pilot who drew aeroplanes did: as he felt deprived of his father, he latched onto his maternal grandfather, who became the hero of his life. However, a grandfather is never a father, and the risk for the child is another form of internal disorganisation. He can imagine that he is his own father, or that his direct genitor is God.

In fact, it is just because of this kind of disorganisation that Peter Pan could whisk off the Darling children on that famous Friday evening. If we observe the scene in a very superficial way, we see children playing in the nursery, and they don't want to go to bed. Or we know that neither children nor adults play at just anything by chance. If we look again more carefully, we see that this particular evening they were playing at 'mothers and fathers'. Were they attempting to find a better kind of organisation than their own parents had achieved?

A little lost girl came to tell me about her sadness, for no one wanted to believe that she was intelligent and capable of growing up. Instead of talking to me about what was hurting her, she invented an imaginary family, and for years we played the game so intensely that we began to believe in their actual existence. Each time I tried to question her or propose an interpretation, she told me to keep quiet. Gradually the little girl grew.

One day she arrived and just dropped into one of the chairs with a big sigh and, looking me straight in the eye for the first time, said: 'Now I want to speak to you.' That day I realised that she had become an attractive adolescent girl. The play family had allowed her to reorganise her feelings, feelings so confused that they prevented her from growing up.

## Betwixt and between of disorganisation

After our escape from Hungary we had to wait several months to reach my father's cherished goal: to leave Europe. Despite his deep cultural roots he was convinced that the Fascist trauma would remain a threat to the Old Continent, so he wanted to move to the New World, where he felt that totalitarian thinking was not necessary.

This period of waiting for the 'great leap' was a perfect time for me. No one went to work or school and we did everything together. In this 'betwixt-and-between' time, just like Peter Pan, it was possible to imagine everything, to play at everything, to be the sun and the air, night and day, little and big, girl and boy, father and mother.

Our first stop was Vienna. It was evening when we arrived, and my father took us directly to his mother's family home; she was of Viennese origin. It was a large apartment in an old building located on the Marokanner Gasse. Its present owner was Paula (the only survivor of the Munks), the maid whom Uncle Hugo had married on his deathbed, much to the outrage of the whole family.

Having recovered from her surprise at our arrival, Paula was not too keen to allow us to stay. My father quickly searched for another solution. He sought help from members of the Scout movement to which he belonged. During his stay in London as an adolescent he had come across Baden-Powell, and was inspired to initiate a Scout group in Hungary with some of his friends. It was thanks to this network that he found places for us to stay. But we were to be separated once again; my mother and I shared a bed at the home of Ida Kraus, who was a widow of tiny stature and a fervent Catholic. My father and brother stayed with another family. Each one of us lost our role just a bit more. Are parents in flight still parents?

When parents have the walls, warmth, and light of a house to help them create a space for childhood, their little ones know that even if they wander off, they will still be able to return to their interior. We were suddenly without a country, without a name, and without a home. During our journey we lived in borrowed interiors belonging to those who were willing to share them with us. Happily, Ida Kraus' hospitality re-created some of the lost sweetness of home.

I still have very clear memories of 'Tante Ida'. I especially liked her smile and her round face; her small size made me feel closer to her. Something unique fascinated me about her apartment: there was a secret room where she retired every evening for long periods. It was generally accepted that this room was forbidden to us, and so my joy was all the greater the day she invited me into her sacred place. I was in such awe that I had to hold my breath: everything inside was gold, silver, and precious stones. There were porcelain dolls in glass cases, and oriental carved wooden boxes of various shapes in all corners of the room. Tante Ida opened one of these and took out a child's ring set with two glittering diamonds with a ruby in the centre. When she took my hand and put the ring on my finger I could hardly believe she was giving me such a precious gift. 'When you wear this ring, you will remember me,' she said, smiling warmly. I flung my arms around her crying, 'I will never forget you!'

Meanwhile my father organised our second escape, crossing from the Russian zone into the American one. 'Tante' Ida's farewell dinner was delightful; she even made a special festive chocolate cake, covered with colourful decorations. It was the first time that I had tasted such a delicacy. What a change from our 'beigli', only made for special occasions.

## Free zone

During the second passage I was aware of it all: the escape and the risks we were taking. Nevertheless, for me it was still an adventure, just like in the movies.

Night had fallen as we set out through the woods on the outskirts of Vienna. The road below was full of Russian soldiers, scanning the forest with powerful spotlights in the hope of catching refugees. As the beams approached we froze and held our breath until they passed by. For me the time seemed endless!

We arrived in Innsbruck at dawn. The free zone at last! During this post-war period Austria was filled with refugee camps called 'lagers', a kind of camp for DPs (displaced persons) without a country, without a passport, without an identity. It was quite natural that we join others who like us had tempted their luck. Nevertheless, the two days in the Innsbruck lager were unbearable. We were allotted a small room in one of the long grey barracks, and given some very rudimentary kitchen supplies. Everything else was shared with the others. People wandered around, listless and sad, the place was shabby and unkempt; my father decided to find another solution. After two days we were given Refugee Status and allowed to leave the camp. We moved to a tiny guesthouse in Innsbruck. Our room was at the end of the corridor, shared with a mother cat and her six kittens. Mother warned me not to handle the kittens as they had just been born. I was nevertheless very happy to watch them for hours.

Our next stop was Salzburg, where I spent the most wonderful, unforgettable moments and experienced the worst fright of my life. Father found us a very comfortable hostel in the wooded hills outside the city just on the edge of the forest. The owners were a family with two children. At first I had little to do with Hans, five years old, and Kristi, nine. I preferred the joy of hiking with my brother every day, discovering hills and valleys, watching out for animals, and picking wild flowers. The smile returned to my father's face as he joined us in the forest, following the tracks that we left for him. At last we felt free. I wanted time to stand still!

Little by little I began playing with Kristi. She had an impressive collection of toys and dolls and she wore the Austrian 'dirndl', the dress of my dreams that was naturally too expensive for me to even hope for. Unfortunately, however, she also had something that frightened me terribly: her aunt! The woman was certainly a very kind person; my father spent hours trying to persuade me without success. Her face was badly deformed by paralysis due to a stroke, and I was convinced she was a witch. One day I stumbled upon her as if in a nightmare.

It was a quiet afternoon, after lunch, Kristi invited me to play with her in her room. 'Come, let's take my new doll's pram out.' She opened the door of the adjoining room and there, lying on the bed, was her aunt! My heart began to race, and my legs weakened. Kristi pushed out the pram; the aunt remained motionless. A few minutes later, however, she came into Kristi's room and advanced directly towards me, holding out her hand to stroke my head and saying 'Kätchen, liebe Kätchen.' I jumped up and ran to the door, trying desperately to open it, pale as a ghost and unable to speak; they let me out at last and I fled to our room. 'Whatever happened?' exclaimed my mother, very surprised. I couldn't reply; I just fainted in her arms.

I have never known that kind of fear since except perhaps a nightmare many years later during my stay at the university residence. One night I woke up in a panic and found myself in the middle of the hallway instead of in my bed. I had dreamt that a giant spider was descending on me.

It is often during moments of passage from one state to another, during important changes, like growing up, for example, that old 'witches' emerge from their boxes to remind us of their presence just when we think they have disappeared for good.

## A visa for the future

In Salzburg we waited for our visas. My father's business contacts in Canada and Australia had agreed to sponsor us as immigrants. During the years following the war these countries needed extra manpower, and it was quite easy to settle as a manual worker. But my father had requested another status. His project was to introduce Hungarian artists to the New World through Christmas and birthday cards that had been very successfully printed by his firm in Budapest. In Canada our sponsor was a Hungarian artist.

Many countries still had to be crossed before reaching the boat for the great voyage. The Zurich train station was impeccably clean, even then; everything sparkled. A colourful little wagon displayed fascinating fruits that I had never seen. As there was still some time before the train pulled out of the station, my father got off and bought two bananas for the four of us to share. It was the most delicious banana I had ever tasted; I could never quite find the same flavour again, even in Africa!

Can one ever rediscover the fragrances of childhood? When the sense of security is lost, the lost child hangs onto the tastes, smells, and pictures of childhood even more intensely. Is it to conserve those delicious hours surrounded by loving parents just for one more moment and be able to come and go without getting lost?

Our next stop was France, where my father had relatives from his mother's side. We arrived in Paris on 14 July 1949; the presence of family made us feel safe again. Furthermore, my father spoke French.

'Pista, why don't you settle in France? Your business contacts are in Europe; you wouldn't be disoriented here …' But my father was determined to proceed with his plans: the way ahead was to go to the New World, to sever his roots and begin all over again. He believed in the promise of a second chance.

Is it possible that I decided then and there, at the age of six, to come back to France one day? Thanks to a seemingly simple event? We were going to cousin Lucie's for dinner, and did some window-shopping on the way in the elegant Trocadero district. I stopped in front of the most beautiful toyshop I had ever seen. Although I didn't dare to ask for anything, it could not stop me from dreaming and thinking about my dolls, my rabbit, lost forever.

The table was already set when we arrived at Lucie's apartment; we waited for her daughter, Nicole. During the war Nicole was captured by the Germans but luckily survived the horrors of the concentration camp. She was seriously traumatised on her return and her mother was very worried about her. She finally arrived carrying a large box; she held out to me. 'Here, this is for you …'

The box, beautifully wrapped in colourful paper, astounded me. In Hungary there was no wrapping of presents. When I finally untangled the bright ribbons and shiny paper to open the box, I couldn't believe my eyes: there was the Little Red Riding Hood doll that I had admired such a short while before in the shop window. I jumped for joy, kissing Nicole and everyone else … I no longer felt alone.

This present must have helped a little to heal the childhood wound that I was carrying. I decided there and then to return to France one day. When I finally did settle in Paris as an adult, it was Nicole who introduced me to the man who was to become my husband and father of our child.

Then the moment came to leave Europe for the New World. We went to Le Havre by train and embarked on the Portuguese ship *San Maria* that was to take us, along with many other emigrants, to Quebec City. I only have a vague memory of our departure, of the land moving away slowly and the people getting smaller and smaller, waving their handkerchiefs sadly as the ship sets out for the open sea.

I know the trip was neither luxurious, nor always pleasant. My neighbour in the bunk-bed, a small four-year-old Russian boy, didn't smile much but chanted from morning till night, 'Banana, banana!' Was our mutual fascination for the exotic fruit a sign of our stressful childhood?

The ship took the northern route, passing near Iceland, and risking the danger of icebergs. My father strolled happily on the deck, speaking to the captain, and other passengers; my mother was worried, full of doubts and questions that remained unanswered. She was already nostalgic for all that she had lost. 'Where are we going to live? Where will you work? What are we going to do with the children?'

For my father these were not important questions; everything would take care of itself when we arrived. Only one thing mattered: 'We are free! Do you realise that we are free?'

## From dream to reality

When we arrived in Toronto, our final destination, the welcome was not exactly as my father had expected. Our 'sponsor' was very nice and polite, but he didn't offer us lodgings while we searched for a place of our own. Instead he reserved a suite for us in one of Toronto's most luxurious hotels. We remained there for a week, after which my father began worrying about finances. We were no longer in a temporary state; there was no question of dreaming about other people's homes.

We therefore changed hotels, transferring to a less elegant district while father searched for more permanent lodgings. It was not easy. Unlike European cities, here many people lived outside the heart of the metropolis in private houses with gardens. It was the poor who lived in shabby buildings in the centre of town not far from the immigrant area where Polish and Russian Jews lived. Many made a living by running used clothes shops, or food stores where you could buy special pickles and other delicacies from Central Europe.

It was in this district that we finally found a Hungarian family of peasant origin. They had immigrated to Canada in the 1930s, making a living by letting rooms in their house. After lengthy negotiations, they agreed to rent to a family with children.

We spent little time in the shabby room; we just cooked our meals and slept there, and that is surely why I have few memories of the place. However, a specific event does come to mind: we were seated at the little table in front of the window having a meal, when suddenly I had an urgent and uncontrollable desire to throw my fork out of the window and see it fly. As a result, I received the only slap on the face that my mother ever gave me!

## Jumping into the void

When a child flees from home with her parents, there is no question of leaving the nursery for there is no longer a nursery, or windows, or parents waiting for the child to return. There only remains the memory of the warmth, of the perfume and the light. There remains only the dream.

Wendy was at that special time in her life when the question of leaving the nursery became real. She needed to be reassured of the strength of her parents, especially of her father. When children reach this critical stage of life they invent all sorts of tricks for testing parental potency to make sure that they can count on them. Sometimes parents are unable to survive this period of testing, and fall into the trap of becoming children themselves. The disappointment of their offspring can be devastating, as with the Darling family.

On that famous yet tragic evening at No. 14, the trap was set with such discretion, and seemed so trivial, that Mr Darling didn't realise the seriousness of it all until afterwards. Let us go and observe the scene in detail, and examine the relevance of the participants' words and gestures. Mrs Darling thinks she sees a little face at the window and is frightened—'My God, my children!'—but the face disappears; everything is normal, the children are playing in the nursery. However, their game is not innocent:

> 'We are doing an act; we are playing at being you and father,' announces John. (He imitates the only father who has come under his special notice.) 'A little less noise in there.'

They play at the most essential scene: parents' desire to have children. Parental desire is not always clear-cut; did they want a girl or a boy? John thinks that one can only want a boy. Wendy is deeply wounded to think that her mother didn't desire her. She thinks that mothers don't care whether it is a boy or a girl, and that they are happy to 'just have a baby!' When it is Michael's turn, John says with a touch of sadism (he is playing Mr Darling's role): 'We don't want any more children; two is enough!' Michael begs desperately: 'Please John, just one more, John, a boy!' He is frightened by the idea that no one wants him. Can one grow up without the assurance of having been wanted by one's parents?

We then meet Mr Darling: he comes on the scene in 'one of those moods that make him incapable of profiting from domestic bliss'. We quickly discover through his words and gestures that he is quite unsure of his authority as a father. That very evening he has a tremendous problem—he cannot tie his cravat! It is of course his wife who must do it for him (as his mother used to?). He searches for her everywhere and is surprised to find her in the nursery with the children, as if he had forgotten about them altogether, and about the fact that he is the father.

Some men have great difficulty in believing in their status as 'father'. One day I received a visit from a young man, seventeen years old, sent by his divorced mother. The apparent reason for his coming was that despite his evident intelligence he was unable to succeed at school. He was a very agreeable young man and used to come to his sessions on roller skates, his way of 'flying' across the city to see me. We rapidly understood that the real reason for his coming was to bring me his father. He needed me to convince his father of his 'fatherhood', for after all he was only seventeen years his senior. He constructed the trap very cleverly, and our work ended when his father finally agreed that his son could live with him.

Mr Darling is so insecure in his role as father that he has to create drama around unimportant events in the hope that this will give him the necessary stature:

> 'I warn you of this, mother, that unless this tie is around my neck we don't go out to dinner tonight, and if I don't go out to dinner tonight, I never go to the office again, and if I don't go to the office again, you and I starve, and our children will be flung into the streets.'

The children are pale with fear as they realise the gravity of the situation.

Mrs Darling knows how to take things in hand; like all good mothers she tries to control the drama that risks destroying her little family: 'Let me try, my dear.'

A terrible silence falls upon their progeny as they cluster around the parents. Will she succeed? Their fate depends on it. She fails—no, she succeeds. In another moment they are wildly gay, romping around the room on each other's shoulders. Father is even a better horse than Mother. Michael is dropped upon his bed, Wendy retires to prepare for hers, and John runs from Nana, who has reappeared with a bath towel.

Everything appears to be back in order. Nevertheless, Michael seems to have some doubts, as he needs to verify with Mrs Darling that she is his mother, and that she still belongs to him: 'Mother, how did you get to know me?' 'At what time was I born, Mother?' 'Oh, Mother, I hope I didn't wake you.'

Alas, parents don't perceive the anxiety behind such words. Mrs Darling finds her son cute and Mr Darling feels the pride of possession: 'Yes, they are cute, aren't they? There is no such thing on earth, and they are ours, ours!'

## Hidden fears

Even if Mrs Darling is deaf to her son's fears, she does recognise the shadow of her childhood apprehensions of Peter Pan breaking into the nursery. She feels guilty about telling her husband; perhaps she knows that he doesn't like to see her act childishly and would be tempted to take advantage of the situation. She tries nevertheless to share her anxiety with him, but in vain:

> 'Cowardy, cowardy custard.'
> 'No, I am not,' she says, pouting.
> 'Oh yes you are.'
> 'George, I am not.'
> 'Then why not tell?'

She is reassured by such common sense. Sliding her hand into his, with the hope that he will protect them from Peter Pan:

> 'George, what can all this mean?'

It is not easy for parents to maintain their role all the time. Some, in fact, never even try; when children come along, they consider them as new playmates! They are often known as 'liberal parents'; in fact they are mothers and fathers who have never been able to leave their own childhood behind.

In the Darling family, Mr Darling seems to be one of these 'father children'. Under these circumstances, the crucial test to see whether father is solid enough is bound to fail. The children's deception, especially that of Wendy, is inevitable.

It all begins when Michael refuses to take his medicine before going to bed. His father tries to reassure him by telling the story of his own childhood:

Mr Darling: 'When I was your age, Michael, I took medicine without a murmur. I said "Thank you, kind parents, for giving me bottles to make me well."'

Wendy, who appears in her nightgown, hears this and believes it.

Wendy: 'That medicine you sometimes take is much nastier, isn't it, father?'

Mr Darling (valuing her support): 'Ever so much nastier. And as an example to you, Michael, I would take it now (thankfully) if I hadn't lost the bottle.'

Wendy (always glad to be of service): 'I know where it is, father. I'll fetch it.'

She is gone before he can stop her. He turns to John who has come in from the bathroom attired for bed.

Mr Darling: 'John, it is the most beastly stuff. It is that sticky sweet kind.'

John (who is perhaps still playing at parents): 'Never mind father, it will soon be over.' A spasm of ill will towards John runs through Mr Darling, and is gone. Wendy returns, panting.

Wendy: 'Here it is father; I was as quick as I could.'

Mr Darling (with sarcasm that is completely lost on her): 'You have been wonderfully quick, precious quick!' He is now at the foot of Michael's bed; Nana is by its side, holding the medicine spoon insinuatingly in her mouth.

Wendy (proudly, as she pours out Mr Darling's medicine): 'Michael, now you will see how father takes it.'

Mr Darling (hedging): 'Michael first.'

Michael (full of unworthy suspicions): 'Father first.'

> Mr Darling: 'It will make me sick, you know.'
>
> John (lightly): 'Come on, father.'
>
> Mr Darling: 'Hold your tongue, sir.'
>
> Wendy (disturbed): 'I thought you took it quite easily, father, saying "Thank you kind parents, for ..."'
>
> Mr Darling: 'That is not the point, the point is that there *is* more in my glass than in Michael's spoon. It isn't fair; I swear though it were with my last breath, it is not fair.'
>
> Michael (coldly): 'Father, I'm waiting.'
>
> Mr Darling: 'It's all very well to say you are waiting; so am I.'
>
> Michael: 'Father's a cowardy custard.'
>
> Mr Darling: 'So are you a cowardy custard.' They are now glaring at each other.
>
> Michael: 'I am not frightened.'
>
> Mr Darling: 'Neither am I.'
>
> Michael: 'Well, then, take it.'
>
> Mr Darling: 'Well, then, you take it.'
>
> Wendy (butting in again): 'Why not take it at the same time?'
>
> Mr Darling (haughtily): 'Certainly. Are you ready, Michael?'
>
> Wendy (as nothing has happened): 'One, two, three.' Michael partakes, but Mr Darling resorts to hanky-panky.
>
> John: 'Father hasn't taken his!' Michael howls.
>
> Wendy (pained): 'Oh father!'

Even if the children in this scene seem to have won in terms of power, since it is they and not their father who show parental force and honesty, they have in fact lost everything. Wendy so wanted her father to be a man; faced with such a tarnished paternal image, a bit of her childhood has been lost. Mr Darling feels that he is diminished in his offspring's esteem. Pretending to make a joke, he takes his revenge on Nana, the dog, by making her drink the medication. This just makes things worse and the children take pity on the poor animal. Mr Darling gives way to his jealousy and chases Nana out of the nursery. One would think that Nana is his rival and that in fact he would like to take her place ...

Mrs Darling, using her maternal intuition, feels that after such an upsetting incident it would be better not to leave the children alone: 'Oh, how I would like to not go out this evening,' she says with a sigh.

Michael, who is so sensitive to his mother's slightest word, starts fretting right away: 'Mother, do you think something could happen to us even if the night lights are on?'

Mrs Darling prefers to keep her own fears and anxieties quiet at this point; 'No, nothing, my darling. Night lights are mother's eyes that she leaves behind her to protect her children.'

## The road to Neverland

Decisive moments in life, those that can turn everything upside down, do not always appear as great adventures. They can present themselves as everyday occurrences that are quickly forgotten. Parents often don't even notice them, even though their children can be transformed by the event.

Mr Darling would never have believed that the little lie concerning the medicine could cost him his children. As he was not very secure in his role as a father, he tried to assert himself by using force unfairly to throw Nana out of the nursery. Unfortunately he was more preoccupied with maintaining his self-image than with being a father capable of keeping his children from tumbling into Neverland.

I think we all have a 'Neverland' somewhere inside us. Some people manage to keep it at a safe distance (with the help of their parents), while others return to it without really knowing why. Describing this internal space is not easy: Neverland is like a map of our minds, with a thousand roads.

Doctors sometimes draw maps of other parts of the body, but drawing a map of a child's mind is another story. Children's thoughts are not only confused, but keep going round all the time. Very similar to Neverland, there are zigzag lines everywhere just like temperature on a card, and these are probably roads on the island; for Neverland is always more or less an island, with astonishing splashes of colour here and there, and coral reefs and rakish-looking craft in the offing, and savages and lonely lairs, and gnomes who are mostly tailors, and caves through which a river runs, and princes with six elder brothers and a hut fast going to decay, and one very small old lady with a hooked nose.

We come at last to meet the Master of Neverland, who swept me away, just like Wendy, John, and Michael, to this place of the spirit where I was able to come close enough to my lost childhood to accept that I should not search for it in reality, but admit its presence inside.

## The little story thief

When we meet him in the nursery, he is a wounded creature who has lost his shadow, but he does not cry for long; he quickly demonstrates how lost children must act, even when they have misplaced their 'double', the only proof of their material existence. Without a shadow, may we wonder if he is only a reflection of his mother's imagination?

This lost child is so light; he has neither name, nor address, nor mother. One immediately wants to comfort him, but stop! He does not want to be touched!

He ignores the meaning of a kiss. He laughs, he plays with what he does not have and he seems very proud of himself. He is ready to do everything to be admired at all costs, to be respected, to exist at last in the eyes of another person, even if he couldn't in those of his mother.

As we get to know him better, we realise that his good, generous, and tender gestures are in fact his way of proving that he exists. The other person is just holding a mirror for him to see himself, and even though she thinks she is indispensable anyone else would do just as well.

Sometimes the mirror is not sufficient proof against the terrible lightness that bears upon the lost child, and he tries other strategies to fill the internal emptiness. That is when he glides into other people's homes, captures the family's heart, and feeds on their intimate stories. Peter, for example, wanted the stories that Wendy had heard in her cradle. He becomes a true pirate, looting other people's treasure.

His great neediness is like a magnet, drawing love and energy to his person, and some people, like Wendy, find him particularly touching. They want to repair the tragedy that seems to lurk behind the childish, baby-toothed smile.

'Boy, why are you crying?' Wendy asks politely.

Even if the lost child allows himself to cry alone from time to time, he must always be smiling when someone else is looking at him: Peter jumps to his feet, approaches Wendy's bed and offers her a graceful bow, using the way of the fairies. He imitates the fairies very well, but he would so like to be like a real child. He therefore asks Wendy her name: 'Wendy Moira Angela Darling,' she answers. He has only one, very light name—'Peter Pan'—and an address that doesn't exist: 'Second star to the right and straight on until morning.'

When Wendy discovers that Peter Pan has no mother, she realises that here is a real tragedy. She jumps from her bed and wants to put her arms around Peter, but he is taken aback suddenly. 'No one must ever touch me!' Is he afraid of feeling something if someone touches him?

Wendy now understands why he was crying a minute ago. Peter denies it of course: 'I was not crying. I can't get my shadow to stick on.'

Peter's shadow, unlike that of most other children, is removable. One wonders if it really belongs to him or whether he found it somewhere on his travels. Is it the shadow of a dead child? I think Peter took the shadow to gain substance as a compensation for his lightness of being.

The proof that he ignores the nature of the shadow is that he thought he could glue it back on simply with soap. Wendy shows him that it has to be sewn on and that it will hurt! Unlike him, she knows her own feelings.

Once the shadow is on, Peter crows like a cock; he is happy and carefree again. Suddenly he seems to need no one and Wendy feels rejected; it is as if she no longer exists for him. He reassures her, the way lost children need reassuring: he flatters her. When a sad child feels a bit lost, it is enough to tell him how wonderful he is, how indispensable he is, to cause him to perk up immediately.

Peter tries this trick on Wendy: 'Wendy, one girl is of more use than twenty boys!' Wendy wants to give him a kiss all of a sudden. Alas, as with so many intimately human things, a kiss is unknown to Peter. Wendy gives him a button instead. Did she understand that for such essential matters it was best to use a substitute?

The lost children who come to see me often discover that their lives have been filled with imitations for many years. For example, a man, unable to love a woman, chooses sports, work, or a dog as the main passions of his life. Love for a real woman involves such serious consequences that the man prefers to invest his feelings elsewhere. He exists on the outside of his life.

Peter is ageless, he 'escaped on the day he was born'. Wendy is curious about his eternal youth and wants to know the reason: 'It is because I heard my father and mother deciding what I was to be when I became a man. I always want to remain a boy and have fun.' A strange way to describe the sad scene of baby Peter locked out of his mother's window, discovering another child in his cradle!

Nevertheless, Peter knows how to render his tragedy attractive to Wendy. He also knows how to flatter her, and assure her that the lost boys (like himself) are in need of 'female company'. 'Oh Peter, it is splendid the way you talk about girls!'

In fact what interests him most of all are the extraordinary fairy tales that she knows. When he discovers that she has even more of them in her head, he becomes very dangerous—he would like to grab them all from her! 'Come,' he says to her, 'I'll teach you how to straddle the wind and away we go! Instead of sleeping in your silly bed at night, you could be flying with me and joking with the stars. There are mermaids, Wendy, with long tails.' She can hardly remain on the nursery floor. 'Come Wendy, you will see how much we respect you!'

With these last words, Peter touches a sensitive chord. Wendy can resist no longer; she lets herself become light and fly off with him.

## The promised land

Canada, a 'frontier' land, was populated by pioneers, accustomed to surviving difficult conditions and to withstanding extremes of nature, climate … and emotions. My father, who had grown up under the reign of Franz Josef, nourished by Mozart, Thomas Mann, and Ady Endre, did not share the same view of life. Furthermore as his name was well known in Hungary, he was surprised to hear people say: 'Who is this guy?' Like Peter Pan, landing in Kensington Gardens, he was neither a bird nor a human being in this new world. What would become of him here? I was unable to ask myself that question back then.

We found new lodgings on the shores of Lake Ontario in the house of an Irish Catholic woman whose name was Dorothy. The memories of that period remain strongly engraved not only in my mind but also in the family's experience. Years later my mother spoke of the times with 'Dorotja' with great contempt.

It was the beginning of our real life in Canada. There was no time now for dreaming; it was about struggling for survival. We, too, had become 'pioneers'. For my father it was urgent to find work; for my brother and me, the moment had come to go to school. Mother's task was to recreate the family atmosphere.

I shall never forget my first day at school. Father took me in the morning. His warm, firm hands reassured me as we walked the long mile together to Corpus Christi, the local Catholic school. I didn't speak a word of English, but my father was sure that I would learn very quickly.

> 'Do you think that children here are the same as in Hungary?'
>> 'How will I reply to the teacher?'
>> 'If I need the washroom, how will I say it?'
>> 'Apu, don't leave me; I'm frightened!'
>> 'I shall come to fetch you after school, don't worry, everything will be fine …'

There I was in the classroom. The teacher, a very young and pretty nun, gave me her hand and showed me to my seat. Her face, without a trace of makeup, shone with cleanliness and internal warmth. I liked her immediately.

'Hi!' said a girl with a friendly smile. Haj (pronounced 'hi') in Hungarian means 'fat, greasy' and I thought of myself as skinny; I didn't understand a thing. At 12 o'clock the bell rang and everyone disappeared in all directions. I did not know that I was to have lunch in the cafeteria, and so I went to the gate to wait for my father. After some time I was the only one left outside the school and I began to panic.

Unable to contain myself, I sobbed desperately. I was lost. A boy from the school, passing by, saw my distress and tried to comfort me. I did not understand anything and began to scream in Hungarian at the top of my lungs. No one could decipher the meaning of this strange language. Happily I was so determined to adapt that it took me only two weeks to learn to speak English. As a result I was considered a gifted child and made to skip the next class!

In Dorothy's house there were nonetheless pleasant moments. Her father, Uncle Bill, liked me; he told me stories and made me toys. Dorothy amused herself by dressing me up and doing my hair in ways that my mother would never even attempt. It was also in this house that I read my first book, *The Adventures of Tom Sawyer*.

Every evening we went for a walk along the boardwalk on the edge of the lake. At that time the area was considered uninteresting as only poor people lived there. Since then all the houses with their wooden verandas have been renovated and are inhabited by university professors in search of peace and quiet. Dorothy's house is still there, as it was, one of the few that has remained unchanged. It looks so small to me now.

The real drama of that period did not trouble me. I would not have understood, although I have the impression that I did feel it. For my parents it was such an enormous shock that we were never able to talk about it, even later on. As with so many other things that happened to us in Canada, this event was 'buried'. We knew about it, we suffered from it, but we preferred not to recall it. We hid it in family history.

Dorothy was having sex with my brother! He was hardly sixteen years old; he was thin, handsome, and very innocent. She was the same age as my mother! As she made herself up, dyed her hair, she looked much younger than my mother, who had aged at least ten years during our adventures.

## A room of my own

We left Dorothy's house immediately. My father succeeded in finding a brand-new apartment in a middle-class neighbourhood in the west end of Toronto. 'You will have a room of your own. We will paint it sky blue, for an angel,' he told me.

My brother's room was light green. Our parents slept in the living room. Father was happy and proud to be able to buy his favourite Scandinavian furniture. Finally we had a place of our own, and could forget all the bad adventures. The fact of having a roof over our heads at last, and rediscovering what it felt like to 'exist' again, gave my parents the hope of being able to reconstruct a new life after all. But I also know that my father was disappointed. Canada was certainly not Europe; cultural life was not as in England. He had toyed with the idea of introducing Hungarian artists to Canadians by producing Christmas cards with their sketches and paintings. However, at the time this style of art did not correspond either to Canadian tastes nor customs, which favoured displays of Santa Claus' robust face and sprigs of holly. No one was interested in 'naïve' Hungarian paintings!

He soon had to give up his dreams and find other work: first of all at a friend's bank, and then with a Dutch printing firm. Printing, his real profession and that of the Kanitz family since 1848, offered some continuity at last! When I went with him to his office, I loved the smell of paper, ink, and pencils; it was just like being back in Hungary.

Sometimes he would come home with new acquisitions, wanting to please and surprise us. One day he brought home an old record player and packages of '45' records, many of which were jazz, including some songs by Bing Crosby and Frank Sinatra. It was pure joy to listen and to dance to the music with my father!

I now attended a public school. I was just like any little Canadian girl; having adapted to the environment, I felt perfectly at ease. At school my best friend was Ruthanne, and in our neighbourhood I became more or less the leader of my 'gang'. I was a real tomboy! My reputation was also enhanced by all the stories I invented. Sometimes we were on an island populated by 'lost boys and pirates' … I was Peter Pan, of course!

## The crab

I don't know exactly how it all happened, but the situation was immediately threatening. One morning my father woke up looking very pale. My mother insisted that he see a doctor at once, but before he could go out he fainted on the doorstep. He had vomited blood during the night.

Memory is strange. My recollection of this moment discontinues, becomes confused … in any case, my father was hospitalised. They thought it was an ulcer, but the fatal word 'cancer' was pronounced very quickly. 'Cancer … cancer of the spine.' In Hungarian the word was 'rak', the crab; it all seemed mysterious to me. What could it be doing in my father's body? Sometimes, however, I had the strange sensation that when he was anxious, something was eating him from inside.

It is only later that the effects of a tragedy emerge in a child. There is no way of knowing how the child will become lost in the drama, and how she will make it her own. Nevertheless, these very personal strategies help form who we are. When I listen to an individual's story I always marvel at the unique, creative methods one uses to cope with life.

Although I was completely helpless when confronted with the calamity that was to take away my childhood forever, something sparked off premature feelings and emotions in me. After the shock of our departure from Hungary, the present circumstances precipitated the moment for my leaving the nursery; like Wendy, I needed to see my father as a man. Suddenly, he interested me in a different way; everything about him fascinated me.

'Mummy, is Father a Jew?' I thought about his nose; it wasn't 'hooked', but a little turned down. I had been told that Jews had hooked noses. We were reading *Oliver Twist* at school; the figure of Fagin was a Jewish caricature. I liked my father's bald head. It shone at the top, and I used to give it a little kiss as I passed by when he was reading in the armchair. I liked his hands. They were slim and neat, with hairs growing at the knuckles. I liked his hairs, and when he took me to the movies I would put my hand on his arm and twirl his hairs into little knots. Sometimes he would lie down on my bed to read me stories. One day, when he was reading *Robinson Crusoe*, and I was lying close to him, I felt a strange electrical impulse going through my body.

The Toronto General Hospital was downtown, and the trip was long and interesting. As one approached the centre of the city, the houses became older, and then gave way to big buildings. It must have reminded me a little of Budapest—I was constantly looking for a smell, a colour, a stone, a street corner from the past.

The hospital was enormous. My mother, although usually without any sense of direction, succeeded in finding the room. I was overwhelmed by the stink of the place and the rows of white beds. I felt a kind of disagreeable nausea rising from my stomach and blocking my throat. Suddenly I was very frightened.

Towards the middle of the large hall, we could identify my father. He was much thinner and he smiled weakly. They had conducted some very painful tests on him, including a coloured injection into his spine. A man was sitting on his bed, a colleague from work. My father's voice was weak.

> 'Yes, there is a tumour, and they must operate. Probably cancerous; I thought that it was only rheumatism. Do you remember how in Austria the toes on my left foot became numb?'
>
> 'Yes, I remember,' said my mother, in a disbelieving tone. 'Cancer! It is not possible; it is not possible!'
>
> 'But you know, a very good doctor is treating me. The Canadians are advanced in this kind of surgery. Everything will be all right; you will see!'

Nothing bad could happen in the 'Promised Land'—there are no negative surprises in 'Neverland', only adventures!

The tests results came a few days later and were positive; my father was operated on immediately. The operation lasted ten hours, and they removed a cancerous tumour from his spine. I can't really remember the days that followed the operation. He was very frail and thin when he came home at last.

## A little mother for Apu

After his return we had to make changes to our apartment, and in our lives. My brother stopped school and became a worker in a large baking factory. The bread was made on a production line; it was white and soft like cotton, and we hated it because we came from a country where bread was brown and had taste. The work was hard; my brother took night shifts and his arms became strong and muscular. He only thought about one thing: buying a Pontiac car so that he could realise the dream that he and my father had created on the boat coming over: 'In Canada we will become rich, we will ride in an American car and visit Niagara Falls!'

My mother was very surprised when my father agreed to let my brother stop school at age sixteen. She thought that his illness must have made him vulnerable. Later on, I understood that other factors prevented him from being a father to his son. One image comes to my mind of that period: my brother rolling on the ground in a rage and my father just watching him, looking sad and shattered. That day I locked myself into the bathroom to pray to God that my brother would not go crazy!

It must have been during the school holidays when Father returned home. I remember staying with him for long hours, while my mother went to work. I made him fried eggs, I cleaned the house, and I played at being a 'little mother' for him. But most important was that I sat for hours at his bedside and we talked at length about everything together.

> 'Apu, tell me about when you were a little boy. What did you like, what did you play with, what did you wear?'
>
> 'Apu how did you meet Anju? Was she beautiful? Did you love her?'
>
> 'And when you were a soldier on a horse? And when you were a prisoner?'
>
> 'Apu, do you think that God exists?'
>
> 'Apu, tell me everything you know.'
>
> 'Apuka, tell-me, tell-me, tell-me.'

He never tired of telling me stories about his childhood, how at the age of six he got up at midnight and crossed the cemetery near their house to prove to himself he was not afraid. He told me about the war, Russia, and how he met my mother. I loved these 'stories' and how he was determined to nourish me with all of it. It was as if he felt the urgency. He wanted to convey everything all at once, things that take a lifetime to tell … everything. I was only ten, and sensitive to the images, the colours, and the vibrations most of all. My father expressed other things as well, but the words were lost, or perhaps I didn't understand them.

At times, when my father was tired, and I wasn't playing at being 'little mother', I simply stayed in my room. It was at one of these moments that I accidentally let the inkwell drop and the dark-blue liquid splashed brutally on the sky-blue wall. I must have cried out, because my father woke up, ran into the room, and began slapping me violently without stopping. I was so staggered I couldn't cry; I had turned into stone. When my father finally came to his senses, he collapsed, and we both cried desperately.

## The crab takes over

After a short respite during which he was able to take on a seemingly normal life, the pain returned. He started to limp and was obliged to go back to the hospital. This time they gave him radiotherapy without any tests to identify the cancer; when the pain became unbearable, they operated again, only to discover that the 'crab' had taken over his whole body.

Again my father came home in an ambulance. He was weaker than before. I don't know why, but this time I didn't play the 'little mother'; I think my mother stayed with him, while I enjoyed myself from morning till night with my 'gang'. I vaguely remember my father saying: 'You are abandoning me this time …'

I must have created a distance to protect myself. In fact I don't remember whether he began working again after this operation. Very soon he was hospitalised at St Michael's Hospital, where people went to die. My mother and I visited him regularly and spent Saturdays and Sundays with him. I still remember all the details of his room; I also recall the depressed faces of the other patients as we walked past them to reach room number 53. My father became very thin, but he still smiled and never complained. 'You know,' he said to my mother, 'I should have taken greater advantage of my life with you. I should have married you earlier! You are the love of my life.' One day he seemed especially happy when we arrived, as if he had found the solution to an important problem.

'Today I spoke to the social worker about Kati's future. She promised that she would assist with her university education.' We never saw the social worker again, but the important thing was that she had been able to give hope to my father. I was passionately devoted to my father's desire; university studies became the main objective of my life.

On Saturdays my mother and I went to the cinema after visiting my father in the hospital. We took sandwiches, and if we found the film interesting we would watch it a second time. This is how we saw

*Gone with the Wind* for six hours! I was very moved by the film, and must have seen it at least thirty times since. At the end I was crying so desperately that my mother had to shake me: 'Kati, Kati, it's only a film, it's only a film!'

Once, after one of these sessions I tried to fix my hair to resemble Scarlett O'Hara, hoping to look beautiful for my father. I started to imagine becoming a woman, and needed my father to approve the test.

When mothers and fathers are steadfast in their parental role so as to assist their children at the difficult moment of leaving the nursery, they unknowingly support them when they face important decisions such as choosing their sex. Just as at birth, when the question of 'boy' or 'girl' is such a determining factor, it is fundamental at this point to understand the difference between 'woman' and 'man'. Without the presence of parents and their calming support, the problem of 'sex' can become enormously difficult for the child. This feeling of having to choose can discourage the lost child from wanting to grow up. If Peter Pan left his home on the day of his birth, it is because he wanted to keep the two choices, between boy and girl. At the end of the story, he cannot bear the fact that Wendy has chosen to become a 'woman'.

My first efforts to leave the nursery were hindered by difficult circumstances. My parents were in a weakened state, and even if I tried to hang on to the memories of my father and his desires for my future, in reality his hands were letting me go, little by little. I therefore turned to my mother and clung to her more and more, rediscovering the very beginning of life. I was like Peter Pan, returning to the window, and my mother let me in, for she also needed to hang on to her daughter, as she would have done with her own mother in such extreme circumstances. I therefore put off the choice of 'sex' for another day, even though I was very curious to know the truth about 'men and women'.

One day a panic-stricken friend in my class told me that her mother was bleeding when she went to the toilet. It frightened me as well, and that evening, as my mother was preparing dinner, I sat in the chair next to the window and told her what was happening to Valerie's mother. 'Do you think she will die? She must be losing all her blood!' My mother started laughing, despite herself. 'It is not an illness, you know, it is quite natural, all women have it. When you grow up you too will bleed every month.'

I was horrified and started to cry. I felt that I had lost something irretrievable, but at the same time an immense curiosity was born in me.

## The last visit

After my father's second operation, we rearranged the apartment once again. My brother slept in my blue room, and my mother and I occupied the room that my parents had shared since the illness. I slept in my father's place; I hold very special memories of that bed.

'Tell me, Anjuka, what men and women do?'
'It is very pleasant … but what is so pleasant?'
'Yes, but with all that I still don't understand how a child can look like his father!'

My mother explained every night. She never got tired of my questions; she didn't mind talking to me about it all. At last I understood, but at the same time I did not really understand.

It was in my father's bed that I had my first menstruation. It was in my father's bed that I cried over his death.

Spring was almost over. The hospital had a park where I would play from time to time when the afternoons became too long in the cancer ward. This particular day my mother sent me to the park and I began picking a bunch of violets for him: 'If I pray very hard, God will surely help him to get well …'

My father could no longer speak. His yellowed skin stuck to his cheekbones, and his tongue seemed so thick that the words had become impossible. He signalled for us to come and kiss him. He was very hot and agitated, as if he saw something that was beyond his grasp. He made signs of blessing with his hands, the only part of his body that remained unchanged, and that was still so familiar to me. My mother sent me to the garden. I kissed my father's hand, without knowing that it would be for the last time.

My brother was in a hurry as usual, and wanted to take us home before his next rendezvous. We left in a rush. I didn't get the chance to give my father the bouquet of violets. My mother was crying. When we arrived home we got a telephone call from the hospital: 'Your husband has just passed away.'

Two days later I answered the phone to a man who knew my father: 'No, he is not here, he is dead.' The man asked to speak to my mother. He congratulated her on having such a brave daughter.

For the funeral ceremony we chose the Hungarian church in the immigrant district of Toronto. First we had to go to the funeral home where the dead are placed to rest among the flowers. I found the odour was worse than that of the hospital. My father's face was transformed. They had blown it up with some fluid, and embellished it with rouge and lipstick to make him look better. The only thing I recognised about him were his hands, still fine and beautiful, hands that had been so warm. It was only in the church when they closed the coffin and the organs began to play that I started screaming with pain and rage. 'Apu, Apu, don't leave me, don't leave me alone; I am terrified!'

We buried him in the new part of a Canadian cemetery, near where we lived. There were no trees. Only the hole in the ground seemed to break the monotony of the land. We lacked the money to buy a gravestone, so my mother, brother, and I constructed a wooden cross out of mahogany; we varnished it with several layers so that it would be resilient. The cemetery refused its installation. Only marble was permitted. Thus my father's tomb remained unmarked, except for a small corner stone where his adopted name was visible. In the beginning I rode my bike to the cemetery to visit my father. Then we moved, and the journey became too far for my bicycle.

# CHAPTER 3

# The past, the passage, and the passer

It is my experience that borders with the past tend to remain blurry. We think we can close the door, not look back, change our identity, but if the passage is disregarded the past continues to prowl like a ghost.

The border we crossed that famous night in 1949, when we left Hungary for Austria, must have disappointed me since it did not function as a 'passage' from one state to another. It left me disoriented probably because I was not old enough for this kind of journey.

Perhaps this is one of the reasons why, when I finally became of age to have a passport and to travel, I never stopped crossing borders: Toronto … Quebec … Paris … London … Geneva … Paris … Bombay … Nairobi … Rio … Tokyo … Sao Paolo … New York … Stockholm … Rome … Paris. I always settled in temporarily; as soon as I began to put down roots, a voice inside told me it was time to move on. So, I had to leave, once again, cross the border, and start anew.

## A name to hide in

My father also thought that he should begin all over again; history provided him with good reasons to try. During World War II, he was shocked and horrified when the Hungarians who knighted his Jewish family (originally from Moravia 400 years earlier) now forced them to wear the yellow star. The Kanitz Printing Firm had served the nation for several generations, and suddenly its owners were being murdered. Three years later, having barely escaped from the hands of one persecutor, he nearly fell into those of another. The uniform and the style were different; instead of Hitler, the newcomer was called Stalin: one assassin had replaced the other.

Once again, we tried to hide. This time, it wasn't in the cupboards or cellars; it was behind a new name. But we ignored that in this new hiding place we would no longer know who we were; we had hidden from ourselves.

Border crossings are fundamental steps in the life of a human being who is passing from one stage to another. These are always difficult times. All cultures and religions have invented rites of passage, not only to make the voyage easier, but also to make sure that there is no possible return. The temptation to go back to the original nest, the mother's womb, may persist. This cannot be done without a guide, often an exceptional person who has directly experienced this ordeal and who has been granted the legal right to bring others across.

The lost child is the one who has not been able to pass: 'All children, except one, grow up …' the lost child. Because the passages were not prepared, or badly prepared, or the guide was not the right one. Or the child passed too early or too late. During such a passage, the child has lost a vital part of the self and is forever looking backwards to try to find it again; he or she is not free to grow up. Fleeing or flying cannot offer passages from one state to another, and hence preclude the possibility of starting anew.

Without passports, bearing a foreign name, accompanied by an illegal escort, we set out for the New World. Thus, without knowing it, we were losing much more than our house on Lake Balaton, our Budapest apartment, and our Kanitz Printing Company. We were losing our Selves. I was small; I looked back, watching my rabbit disappear, while installing the Neverland of my childhood deep in my heart. As for my father, he did not survive this exodus.

When the passage is not mastered, when the transformations are not clear, the past permeates the present, and the future begins to resemble the past. The difference between the sexes and of generations tends to merge: parents lose their role, and children play at being the parents of their own parents.

In this kind of blurred situation the only alternative is 'for or against' … 'kill or be killed' … 'eat or be eaten'. Life loses all its complexity, and one no longer distinguishes differences. This extreme simplification may remind us of our origins, the 'very beginning' when nothing exists outside 'mother' and 'not mother'; her presence or her absence so vital for the newborn baby.

Peter Pan's Neverland bore a strange resemblance to all this. The question remains: was the passage of Wendy, John, and Michael to Neverland truly a passage to growing up, or was it just another adventure of no importance? Was it a step forward, or a big somersault backwards? I am inclined to favour the somersault, even though it had no tragic consequences for Wendy (as for her brothers, we do not know).

Peter Pan possessed none of the characteristics of a guide. He was a lost child, deeply wounded, who sought refuge in Neverland because he could not do otherwise. He brought the Darling children with him, not at all for the purpose of growing up (which is often the purpose of fairy tales). In fact, he almost lost them on the way; he was such an inattentive guide. He decided to bring them along only for his own personal needs to take from them what he most lacked: a mother.

## On the wings of the wind

Those who claim not to know Neverland are mistaken, because we have all been there some time or other, even if only fleetingly.

It is true that in growing up we watch the little island of our childhood recede into the distance, become misty and pale, and we might imagine it going out like a waning candle. But sometimes it only takes a certain scent, a ray of sun dancing on a white wall, a note of music, or a simple street corner, for Neverland to reappear, and for us to be catapulted backwards to where time does not exist.

When this happens, everything becomes possible again. We are at once air and breath, water and drinker, king and queen, boy and girl. We can be both here and there at the same time. We can speak or be silent, because we are always understood. With the bat of an eye, we can transform ourselves into someone else: father, mother, brother, or sister; we are all equal. But the master of the island must always be at the centre.

During the day we can have hundreds of adventures in Neverland and emerge as the hero each time. But at nightfall suddenly the island's scenery assumes new contours. Familiar objects appear bizarre, and wild animals emerge from their lairs. The queen turns into a huge tentacular spider. Father and mother disappear, and we are suddenly tiny and defenceless. Some people have known Neverland at night, and prefer to forget it. Others return to it with great pleasure, to re-experience the child they left behind, whose memory becomes indispensable for the continuity of living.

'Second star to the right, and then straight on till morning!' Those were Peter's instructions to Wendy for the way to Neverland, but even birds, carrying maps and consulting them at windy corners, could not have sighted it with these directives. Peter just said anything that came into his head.

At first his companions had absolute confidence in him, so great was their delight in flying. They wasted time circling around church spires or any other tall objects that took their fancy. Sometimes it was dark, and sometimes light, and now they were very cold and again too warm. Did they really feel hungry at times, or were they merely pretending because Peter had such a strange new way of feeding them? His way was to pursue birds that had food in their mouths suitable for humans and snatch it from them. But Wendy noticed with gentle concern that Peter did not seem to know that this was rather an odd way of getting your bread and butter, nor even that there are other ways.

There were certainly many things that Peter did not know, and this was surely why he had insisted on taking Wendy and her brothers to Neverland. His visits to the window of No 14 enabled him to see how real children act when they have a mother all to themselves, who watches them growing up. It is difficult to grow up without a mother's gaze.

What could Wendy teach Peter? Did he simply want her to look at him through a mother's eyes? On the way he never stopped boasting; for instance, Peter would fly close to the water and touch each shark's tail in passing … (the children) were incapable of playing this game and were certain that he was doing this for the show, especially as he kept looking behind to make sure that they admired him.

## Memory lapses

Sometimes he left them alone. This enabled him 'to have an adventure' in which they had no share. He would come down laughing over something fearfully funny he had been saying to a star, but he had already forgotten what it was, or he would come up with mermaid scales still sticking to him and yet not be able to say for certain what had happened. It irritated the children especially as they had never seen a mermaid.

'And if he forgets them so quickly,' Wendy argued, 'how can we expect him to remember us?'

Indeed, sometimes when he returned, he did not remember them, at least not well. Wendy was sure of it. She saw recognition come into his eyes as he was about to pass by them. 'I'm Wendy,' she said agitatedly.

He was very sorry. 'I say, Wendy,' he whispered to her 'always if you see me forgetting you, just keep on saying, "I'm Wendy," and then I'll remember.'

This was rather unsatisfactory, of course. To make amends, however, he showed them how to lie out flat on a strong wind that was going their way, and this was such a pleasant change that they tried it several times and found they could sleep on their back quite safely. Indeed, they would have slept longer, but Peter tired quickly of sleeping, and shouted in his Captain's voice, 'We get off here.'

Peter's lapses of memory are an indication of his deep sadness and of his inability to truly connect with anyone. The children interest him because he believes he can feed on their substance as 'real children'. But as soon as his attention is diverted by something else, it is as if he were totally unaware of their existence.

Curiously, Neverland was not unknown to the Darling children: 'Wendy, look at the turtles, burying their eggs in the sand.' 'I say, John, I see your flamingo with the broken leg.' 'Look, Michael, there's your cave.' Peter was a little annoyed with them for knowing so much. Yet the time came when Neverland began to look dark and threatening.

Then unexplored patches arose in it and spread; black shadows moved about in them; the roar of the beasts of prey was quite different now, and above all you lost the certainty that you would win. You were quite glad that the nightlights were on. You even liked Nana to say that this was just the mantelpiece over here and that Neverland was all make-believe … but it was real now, and there were no nightlights, and it was getting darker every moment, and where was Nana?

A mother's role is to be present when the dangerous side of Neverland approaches. Her closeness helps the child to gain sufficient self-confidence to become brave and believe that he/she can succeed until this becomes a reality. Once one is an adult, Neverland seems less dangerous.

Deprived of his mother's gaze, Peter had to face Neverland alone. This is why his terrible side could appear at any moment. This did not seem to overly upset him.

For example, death did not bother him: 'There's a pirate asleep in the pampas just beneath us,' he explained to John. 'If you like, we'll go down and kill him.'

Peter tried to make the children believe that killing a pirate was no more serious than having a cup of tea, and he promised them great adventures to look forward to. When they discovered that the Pirate Captain was none other than the terrible 'Captain Hook' and that Peter had cut off his right hand to feed the crocodile, the children immediately imagined the scale of terror that reigned over the island.

Peter remained unperturbed when John, panic-stricken, whispered huskily: 'He has an iron hook instead of a right hand, and he claws with it?' 'Exactly!' replied Peter.

## Captain sad

Kill or be killed is the basic rule of the island. The other imperative is never to grow up, nor say the word 'mother'. The two captains of course are Peter Pan, the leader of the lost boys, and Captain Hook, the chief of the pirates. Are they not one and the same person? Hook is the saddest of the sad children, whereas Peter Pan is young, innocent, and heartless. Hook is old and sinister, but also heartless. Since Peter cut off Hook's hand and fed it to the crocodile, Hook's situation has deteriorated.

He already had a very bad self-image, but this amputation inflicted a deep wound on his soul as well as on his body.

Hook's manner of speaking is that of a man educated in the best British schools. Like Mr Darling, he is hypersensitive to other people's opinions of him. He finds Peter Pan's self-assurance unbearable, something that he himself has lost and wants so much to recapture. Let us take a closer look at him.

> He lay at his ease in a rough chariot, drawn and propelled by his men, and instead of a right hand he had the iron hook with which ever and anon he encouraged them to increase their pace. As dogs this terrible man treated and addressed them, and as dogs they obeyed him. In person he was cadaverous and dark-skinned, and his hair was dressed in long curls, which at a distance looked like black candles and made him look particularly threatening. His eyes were as blue as forget-me-nots, but profoundly melancholy, save when he was plunging his hook into you, when two red spots appeared and lit them up horribly. In manner, something aristocratic still clung to him. He could be extremely charming, and I have been told that he was a raconteur of repute. He was never more sinister than when he was most polite, which is probably the truest test of breeding, and the elegance of his diction, even when he was swearing, no less than the distinction of his demeanour, showed him one of a different cast from his crew. A man of indomitable courage, it was said of him that the only thing he shied at was the sight of his own blood, which was thick and of an unusual colour …

Such is the terrible man against whom Peter Pan is pitted. Who will win?

The lost child sometimes has a father Hook. The father, himself profoundly sad, digs his hook into his son, and grasps onto a young double of himself, presenting him with a picture of a wounded, passive creature. This child is thus prevented from living his own life, and cannot but identify with a wounded, sick paternal image. Is he doomed to transmit the same?

An athletic young man suffering from violent stomach pains came to consult me. Since doctors had dismissed any medical reasons, his pain obviously stemmed from something else. He could not understand the cause of his suffering because he led an ordinary, uneventful existence, yet this problem prevented him from enjoying the pleasures of life: his academic success, music, and dance. He rarely went out with women, and only allowed himself affairs with those who were already attached. From time to time he tried to end his suffering by practising dangerous sports such as hang-gliding and rock climbing in which he risked his life, but this never worked. Whenever he was successful, he would lose pleasure in the activity.

From our very first session he spoke about the difficult relationship he had with his father, a quiet man discontented with life, who never played with him. At the age of five, he received a train for Christmas and didn't want to open the package, hoping that his father would play with him. But his father remained as passive as ever, and the little boy never opened the box!

One day the image of his father emerged in the session: he was sad, alone, smoking a cigarette, and waiting to resume the work he hated. This pathetic tableau, full of emotion, returned and dug into him like a hook: 'He's the one who prevents me from living, the bastard,' the young man cried out on discovering this painful, tormented father in the pit of his stomach. After that session the battle continued for a long time and the question, 'Who will win, father or me?' weighed heavily throughout our work.

## Because of the crocodile

Neverland always includes a crocodile; therefore, the strategy of Peter Pan is not easy to adopt. I have known some sad children like this who, as soon as they feel better and dare to laugh again, the crocodile reappears to persecute them. The next day, they are sadder than before.

One possible alternative for them is to raise a dog or a wild animal. The crocodile then remains outside and cannot get inside the person. The dog or wild animal tends to bite others, and be faithful and gentle to his master. Once a friend's dog bit me, and she apologised with the following: 'He only bites people I like!'

Captain Hook did not have a moment of peace between Peter Pan, who pursued him, and the crocodile, which hunted him down everywhere. From then on confrontation was inevitable. The opportunity was provided by the capture of Peter's friend Tiger Lily, the little Indian girl: two of Hook's men captured Lily and dragged her, solidly bound with cords, into their boat. They were ordered to abandon her on Mariner's Rock, to be drowned when the tide rose.

Quite near the rock, but out of sight, two heads were bobbing up and down, Peter's and Wendy's. Wendy was crying; for it was the first tragedy she witnessed. Peter had seen many tragedies, but he had forgotten them all. He was less sorry than Wendy for Tiger Lily: it was two against one that angered him, and he intended to save her.

An easy way would have been to wait until the pirates had gone, but he was never one to choose the easy way.

Clearly, it is simpler to defend principles than it is to experience feelings! He therefore decided to imitate Hook's voice and order the pirates to release Tiger Lily. This worked like a charm, because something he loved to do, and always did best, was to imitate someone else. Was he beginning to slide into Hook's skin?

In any case, the pirates obeyed and cut Tiger Lily's cords, at the very moment when the real Hook swam to the boat.

In the light of the lantern Wendy saw his hook grip the boat's side; she saw his evil swarthy face as he rose dripping from the water. Captain Hook sighs sadly, and says in desperation: 'The game's up … those boys have found a mother!'

Hook can only pursue his evil schemes in the absence of a 'mother'.

## Identity

But Peter did not enjoy the success of his ruse for long, because the Pirate Captain began to suspect something:

> 'Spirit that haunts the dark lagoon tonight,' he cried, 'dost hear me?' Of course, Peter should have kept quiet, but he did not. He immediately answered in Hook's voice: 'Odds, bobs, hammer, and tongs, I hear you.' In that supreme moment Hook did not blanch, even at the gills, but Smee and Starky clung to each other in terror.
>
> 'Who are you, stranger, speak?' Hook demanded.
>
> 'I am James Hook,' replied the voice, 'Captain of the Jolly Roger.'

'You are not,' Hook cried hoarsely.

Hook tried a more ingratiating manner. 'If you are Hook,' he said almost humbly, 'come tell me, who am I?'

'A codfish,' replied the voice, 'only a codfish.'

'A codfish!' Hook echoed blankly.

And it was then, but not till then, that his proud spirit broke. He saw his men draw back from him.

'Have we been captained all this time by a codfish!' they muttered. 'It is lowering to our pride.'

But … he scarcely heeded them. Against such fearful evidence it was not their belief in him that he needed, it was his own. He felt his ego slipping from him. 'Don't desert me, bully,' he whispered hoarsely to it.

In his dark nature there was a touch of the feminine, as in all the great pirates, and it sometimes gave him intuitions. Suddenly he tried the guessing game.

'Hook,' he called, 'have you another voice?'

Now Peter could never resist a game, and he answered blithely in his own voice, 'I have.'

'And another name?' 'Aye, aye.'

'Vegetable?' asked Hook.

'No.'

'Mineral?'

'No.'

'Animal?'

'Yes.'

'Man?'

'No!' This answer rang out scornfully.

'Boy?'

'Yes.'

'Ordinary boy?'

'No!'

'Wonderful boy?'

To Wendy's pain the answer that rang out this time was 'Yes … Can't guess?' crowed Peter. 'Do you give up?'

Of course, in his pride he was carrying the game too far, and the miscreants saw their chance.

'Yes, yes,' they answered eagerly.

'Well, then,' he cried, 'I am Peter Pan.'

'Pan!'

This declaration changed everything for Hook. Strange to say, he had both to destroy and preserve the image of the wonderful boy, so that he himself could be something other than a poor codfish. A father Hook needs the presence of his son; the only justification for a life without pleasure is to be able to transmit his wound.

## Painful injustice

Henceforth the confrontation was inevitable.

It was not in the water that they met. Hook rose to the rock to breathe, and at the same moment Peter scaled it on the opposite side. The rock was slippery as a ball, and they had to crawl rather than climb. Neither knew that the other was coming. Each feeling for a grip met the other's arm: in surprise they raised their heads; their faces were almost touching.

One may have thought that Peter would be afraid at this moment.

But Peter had one feeling only, delight. And he gnashed his pretty teeth with joy. Quick as a thought, he snatched a knife from Hook's belt and was about to drive it home, when he saw that he was higher up the rock than his foe. It would not have been fighting fair. He gave the pirate a hand to help him up. It was then that Hook bit him.

Peter was dazed not by the pain he felt but its unfairness. It made him quite helpless. He could only stare, horrified. Every child is affected, the first time he is treated unfairly. All he wants when he comes to you, to be yours, is fairness. After you have been unfair to him, he will love you again, but he will never be quite the same boy. No one ever gets over the first unfairness, no one except Peter. He often met it, but he always forgot it. I suppose that was the real difference between him and everyone else.

So, when he faced it now it was like the first time. He could just stare, helpless. Twice, the iron hand clawed him. Peter, wounded, remained alone on the rock, which became very small now; soon it would be submerged. Pale rays of light tiptoed across the waters, and by and by there was to be heard a sound at once the most musical and the melancholiest in the world: the mermaids calling to the moon.

Peter was not quite like other boys, but he was afraid at last. A tremor ran through him, like a shudder passing over the sea, but on the sea one shudder follows another until there are hundreds of them, and Peter felt just the one. The next moment he was standing erect on the rock again, with that smile on his face and a drum beating within him. It was saying, 'To die will be an awfully big adventure.'

'To die will be an awfully big adventure': these words distinguish Peter from the other children, and they betray the depth of his sadness. When the inability to feel is powerful enough to extinguish even the fear of death, it means that the child can go no further in desolation and despair. Since he is capable of playing with what he does not have, his very life becomes the challenge of a great adventure.

## Pretending

Everything was play in Neverland. The favourite game of the lost boys and the Darling children was 'fathers and mothers'. Wendy acted the 'little mother' to perfection, and Peter obviously took the role of 'father'. One day, this game felt too close to reality and disturbed him; he was not sure whether he was awake or asleep.

> 'Peter, what is it?'
>
> 'I was just thinking,' he said, a little scared. 'It is only make-believe, isn't it, that I am their father?'
>
> 'Oh, yes,' Wendy said primly … 'Peter,' she asked, trying to speak firmly, 'what are your exact feelings for me?'
>
> 'Those of a devoted son, Wendy.'
>
> 'I thought so,' she said, and went and sat by herself at the extreme end of the room.

Peter was perfectly sincere; he was incapable of imagining what women could expect of him, except to protect him by creating a very comfortable home for him.

Is it possible for a man to love a woman when he lives with his father's hook in the pit of his stomach? Like Peter, this son tends to be passive towards a woman, to treat her like a mother, because if he permitted himself to desire her sexually he would be afraid of killing her. Sexual desire is a blend of aggressiveness and tenderness; when tenderness is paralysed, aggressiveness becomes murderous.

As time passes, sad children realise that it is no longer possible to pretend by playing 'fathers and mothers'. They gradually come to understand that a love story between a man and a woman is a very serious matter, and that it can hurt.

One day a man came to tell me his story. Listening to him, I was struck by the idea that this man had never experienced love with a woman, despite two marriages and many affairs. Though I am not in the habit of asking intimate questions directly, I suddenly said: 'Have you ever loved a woman?' He gazed at me somewhat surprised, reflected and then answered: 'No, never.'

Few men and women succeed in being so honest with themselves on such questions. Yet sad children, when they find themselves marooned in an adult's body, often come to ask for advice. For although they can make-believe for themselves, it may not work when it concerns their partners.

Sometimes the man, Peter Pan, finds a Wendy ready to accept everything; however, when Wendy tires and leaves her Peter, he is completely lost, having understood nothing of what happened between them.

Was Wendy disappointed in Peter as she had been previously with her father? Was it disillusion that made Wendy decide to leave Neverland? In any case, she felt that there was no shortcut to growing up. Pretending to be a mother would not help her to become one. It sometimes happens to women, who have not yet completed their childhood, to decide to have a child in the hope that this will make them grow up. Alas, the baby placed in this situation is liable to respond to the deep needs of its mother, in other words forced to play the maternal role, from the day he is born.

Wendy realised that she still needed her real mother to be able to become a mother herself one day. The thought was accompanied by a new awareness: her mother might be anxious about her absence. For the first time she allowed herself to experience her mother's feelings. Was it a step towards motherhood? All this was possible for Wendy because she knew that the love of a mother is infinite. Unlike Peter, she was convinced that her mother had left the window open for her children to return. She repeated this confidently in the story she told the children every night.

At the same time she violated the rules of Neverland. By allowing her true mother to enter (a way of accepting her origins), she also introduced time—in other words, the future.

## The eyes of a mother

'Did they ever go back?' asked one of the lost boys.

'Let's now, take a peep into the future.' replied Wendy. They all twisted themselves to get a better look.

'Years have rolled by … See, dear little ones,' says Wendy, pointing upwards, 'there is the window still standing open. Ah, now we are rewarded for our sublime faith in a mother's love.' So up they flew to their mummy and daddy, and pen cannot describe the happy scene, over which we draw a veil.

But Peter was so disturbed by this story that he decided to unveil his secret, the tragedy of his life:

'Long ago,' he said, 'I thought like you that my mother would always keep the window open for me; so I stayed away for moons and moons and moons, and then flew back; but the window was barred, for mother had forgotten all about me, and there was another little boy sleeping in my bed.'

'Wendy, let's go home,' cried John and Michael together.

So, you can see that the decision to leave Neverland can be taken quickly, only once the right time has come. Wendy was ready to bring everyone back to real life, where mothers are mothers and children are children … but Peter refused to follow them.

To show that their departure would leave him unmoved, he skipped up and down the room, playing cheerily on his heartless pipes. 'To find your mother,' she coaxed.

Now, if Peter had ever quite had a mother, he no longer missed her. He could do very well without one. He had given 'mothers' considerable thought and remembered only their bad points.

A lost child said to me one day: 'I miss my mother terribly,' and I felt that nothing more horrifying could happen to her. Often, a lost child can only express negative feelings about the mother. For example, a young woman, whom I saw over a number of years, never tired of telling me how badly her mother had treated her. The 'appalling' thing was that she had sent her at the age of three, to live with her grandmother for a seemingly long time. The daughter, unable to identify the 'wound', invented a witch of a mother, on whom she could spit her venom. Later on, when she had sorted it out, her mother became a wonderful and loving person again.

Nothing and no one in the world could persuade Peter to leave Neverland, because he clung so strongly to the negative image of his mother. It was his most precious possession.

One sometimes feels that the child can detach himself more easily when the image of the mother is negative. Often, the very opposite occurs, and the child never succeeds in getting away. The man who could not love a woman said one day that he felt the presence of his mother everywhere. Although she had been dead for years, he had the impression she was lurking behind every door. Such a mother can only obstruct the road to love, as all the son's energy is invested in resisting her!

## Departure from Neverland

Neverland is not dismantled easily; it never vanishes without a fight! Though Peter didn't want to follow the children, he pretended to help them in their plans for departure; this moment of inattention enabled Hook to achieve his sinister plan. Taking advantage of the fact that no one was thinking about the pirates, he succeeded in capturing the children and dragging them to his ship! In Neverland one cannot be sure of anything; the most terrible conflicts can break out in a single instant of distraction, especially if a change is underway.

When Peter Pan learned that Wendy and the lost boys were captured, he swore to rescue them. He took a terrible oath: 'Hook or me this time!'

Captain Hook paced the deck unsteadily, submerged by his success. Despite his apparent triumph, there was no elation in his step;

the rhythm was tuned to his tortured spirit. Hook was in fact profoundly depressed.

He was often thus when communing with himself on board ship in the quietude of the night. It was because he was so terribly alone. This inscrutable man never felt more alone than when surrounded by his 'dogs'.

Peter, convinced of ruling Neverland, found the way to triumph over Hook. Once again, he resorted to his strategy of imitation: he slid into the skin of the crocodile. He had seen the crocodile pass by without noticing anything peculiar about it, but then he remembered that it had not been ticking … What happened to the clock it had swallowed?

Without giving a thought to the feelings of a fellow creature thus abruptly deprived of its closest companion, Peter at once considered how he could turn the catastrophe to his own use; and he decided to tick … and ticked superbly.

With this new identity, he climbed aboard the ship easily and hid in the cabin, like a monster in the ignoble belly of the colossus. From there, he started ticking in order to terrify his enemy.

The change that came over Hook was frightful! It was as if he had been clipped at every joint. He fell in a little heap … Even the iron claw hung inactive … He crawled on all fours on his knees along the deck as far from the sound as he could go. The pirates respectfully cleared a passage for him … 'Hide me,' he cried hoarsely. They gathered around him … but they had no thought of defending him.

Hook was faced with his fate. Fate, crocodile, Peter …

In the meantime, Peter had released the boys. Only Wendy was still bound to the mast. Peter cut Wendy's bonds and took her place by the mast. This new change of identity enabled him to surprise the pirates. The battle was set: Hook and Peter were face to face.

The others drew back and formed a ring about them. For a long time the two enemies looked at one another; Hook shuddering slightly, and Peter with a strange smile upon his face.

'So, Pan,' said Hook at last, 'this is all your doing.'
'Aye, James Hook', came the stern answer. 'It is all my doing.'
'Proud and insolent youth', said Hook. 'Prepare to meet thy doom.'
'Dark and sinister man,' Peter answered, 'take this!'

Without another word, they crossed swords!

They only stopped when Peter had wounded Hook, piercing him in the ribs.

At the sight of his own blood, whose peculiar colour, you remember, was offensive to him, the sword fell from Hook's hand, and he was at Peter's mercy …

'Pan, who and what art thou?' he cried huskily.

'I'm youth, I'm joy,' Peter answered at once. 'I'm a little bird that has broken out of the egg.'

It was absurd of course, but it was proof for the miserable Hook that Peter had no idea of who he really was.

Hook had to admit that his final moment had come. Seeing Peter slowly advancing upon him through the air with dagger poised, he sprang upon the bulwarks to cast himself into the sea. He did not know that the crocodile was waiting for him …

That night, the lost boys slept in the pirates' bunks; all but Peter, who strutted up and down on deck until at last he fell asleep … Afterwards he had a nightmare and Wendy had to hold him very tight in her arms as he was crying in his sleep.

## The return home

The window was open at No. 14, just as it was every night, to welcome the children. The beds were ready and Mr Darling had fallen asleep, as usual, in Nana's kennel. Since the children had left, he had decided that that was his place. That would teach him for being jealous of a dog!

As for Mrs Darling, she had lost her former gaiety. Was it her fault if she was too fond of her children? It was so sad to see her in her chair, where she had fallen asleep, looking so miserable. Her hands moved restlessly on her chest as if she had a pain there.

Peter reached the window first, and he closed it quickly to make Wendy believe that her mother had barred her out. But then he saw the tears in Mrs Darling's eyes.

'She wants me to unbar the window,' thought Peter, 'but I won't, not I.'

He peeped again, and the tears were still there—or another two had taken their place.

'She's awfully fond of Wendy,' he said to himself. He was angry with her now for not seeing why she could not have Wendy. The reason was simple: 'I'm fond of her too. We can't both have her, lady.'

But the lady would not give up. He forced himself not to look at her, but even then she would not let go of him. He skipped about and made funny faces, but when he stopped it was just as if she were inside his heart, knocking on the partition. 'Oh, all right,' he said at last, and gulped. Then he unbarred the window.

'Come on, Tink,' he cried, with a frightful sneer at the laws of nature, 'we don't want any silly mothers,' and he flew away.

No sooner had they landed in their room than the children slipped into their own beds, although the youngest had some difficulty recognising his own. Mrs Darling's surprise was even greater to discover them asleep in their beds; she called her husband and Nana to share her bliss.

There could not have been a lovelier sight, but there was none to see it except a strange boy who was staring in at the window. He had ecstasies innumerable that other children can never know, but he was looking through the window at the one joy from which he must be forever barred.

## Spring cleaning

When they heard about the lost boys, Mr and Mrs Darling immediately agreed to adopt them. This left Peter. Mrs Darling proposed to adopt him too, but when he learned that the condition of this was to become a man, he refused point-blank. He simply wanted Wendy to return with him to Neverland. She begged her mother to let her go, as if she felt unable to resist again: 'But he does so need a mother.' 'So do you, my love.'

They finally struck a compromise. Wendy would go to him for a week every year to do his spring cleaning. She preferred a more permanent arrangement, and it seemed to her that spring would be long in coming, but this promise sent Peter away quite gay again. He had no sense of time, and was so full of adventures …

Wendy must have known this when she said to him: 'You won't forget me, Peter, will you?' Of course not, Peter promised; then he flew away. He took Mrs Darling's kiss with him. The kiss that even Wendy could not have, Peter took quite easily. Funny. But she seemed satisfied … At the end of the first year Peter came to get Wendy. She flew away with him in the frock she had woven from leaves and berries in Neverland. Her one fear was that he might notice how short it had become; but he never noticed, he had so much to say about himself. She was also impatient to talk with him about old times, but too many new adventures had crowded the old ones from his mind.

> 'Who is Captain Hook?' he said with interest when she spoke of the arch-enemy.
>
> 'Don't you remember,' she asked, amazed. 'How you killed him and saved all our lives?'
>
> 'I forget them after I kill them,' he replied carelessly.

To avoid suffering, the lost child is forced to 'kill' memories charged with great emotion. The young sportsman unable to enjoy the pleasures of his life told me that there was a kind of 'fog' that prevented him from feeling. A long time ago he had experienced such unbearable emotions that he was forced to destroy them. 'See nothing, hear nothing, feel nothing,' he said.

To please Peter, Wendy tried not to grow up too fast; she even felt that she had cheated on him when she received first prize in the general knowledge contest.

Many years went by before the careless boy deigned to reappear. When they next met she had become a woman. She was married and Peter was no more to her than a little dust in a box in which she had kept her old toys. You need not be sorry for her; she was the kind who likes to grow up.

She had a daughter who was called Jane, and who loved to hear her mother tell her all she could remember about Peter Pan and the fabulous flight:

> 'The way I flew! Do you know, Jane, I sometimes wonder whether I ever did really fly.'
>
> 'Yes, you did.'
>
> 'The dear old days when I could fly!'

## The betrayal

The tragedy arrived unexpectedly one night … after the bedtime story had been told, and Wendy was sitting on the floor, very close to the fire … The window blew open as of old, and Peter dropped to the floor.

He was exactly the same as ever, and Wendy saw at once that he still had all his first teeth. She huddled by the fire not daring to move, helpless and guilty of being such a big woman.

'Hello, Wendy,' he said, not noticing any difference, for he was thinking chiefly of himself; in the dim light her white dress might have been the nightgown in which he had seen her first.

'Hello, Peter,' she replied faintly, squeezing herself as small as possible. Something inside her was crying 'Woman, woman, let go of me'.

Peter looked for the two boys in the beds, and Wendy was forced to say:

'That is not Michael.'

Peter looked.

'Hello, is it a new one?'

'Yes.'

'Boy or girl?'

'Girl.'

Wendy realised that he was expecting her to fly away with him. But even when she told him that she could no longer fly, he didn't want to know. She rose, and now at last a great fear assailed him.

'What is it?' he cried, shrinking.

'I will turn up the light,' she said, 'and then you can see for yourself.'

For the first time in his life that I know of, Peter was afraid. 'Don't turn up the light,' he cried.

With a sudden surge of emotion, she caressed the hair of the tragic boy. She was no longer a little girl heartbroken about him; she was a grown woman smiling at it all, but her smiles were humid.

Then she turned up the light, and Peter saw. He gave a cry of pain, and when the tall, beautiful creature stooped to lift him in her arms, he drew back sharply.

'What is it?' he cried again.

She had to tell him. 'I am old, Peter. I am ever so much more than twenty. I grew up long ago.'

'You promised not to!'

'I couldn't help it. I am a married woman … and the little girl in the bed is my baby.'

'No, she's not.'

But he knew that it was the truth because he drew his sword, ready to strike. Of course, he did nothing of the sort, and instead he sat down on the floor and sobbed; Wendy, who before had known what to do, was at a complete loss at how to comfort him. She was only a woman now, and she ran out of the room to try to think.

Peter continued to cry, and soon his sobs woke Jane. She sat up in bed …

No need to say more; it is easy to picture what happened!

## Never grow up

Poor little sad child! Is he still the hero of Neverland or has he become its prisoner? The enigma of the story remains intact: Wendy used it to help her grow up, while Peter was doomed to repeat adventures and battles forever. Even if the actors change, their roles remain identical.

The last picture, that of the little boy sobbing at the feet of the grown woman, recalls the image of baby Peter Pan beating on the windowpane. Behind the window is the mother, without whom one cannot grow up. Peter stands in front of an unreachable mother like a child by the coffin of a dead parent.

One crucial question remains: how did Wendy succeed in leaving Neverland while Peter has remained there forever? We witnessed how a disenchantment, a moment of sadness, a loss of illusion was enough to make these two children vanish into Neverland, where everything is possible.

Peter pretends that it was his decision to leave his parents on the day of his birth; he does admit that he tried to return, but that he was unwanted. This parental rejection determined his entire life, and one suspects that if he ever became an adult, he would resemble Captain Hook, because he too knows about self-hatred.

Does he really think that Wendy's presence will change things in Neverland? He counts on Wendy's love to replace the love of his own mother? Does he believe that thanks to this love, he will be able to love himself? Yet we know that Solomon Caw told him there was no second chance.

For Wendy, Neverland has another function. Her disappearance serves as a lesson to her parents: for her father, because he lied, and for her mother, her rival, because she did not protect her from paternal deceit. Yet to disappear in this way, the child must have implicit trust in her parents and in their love. Quite often, children who 'cling' most to their mothers are those who are afraid of being abandoned.

When Wendy reaches Neverland, she already has a sexual identity. She has crossed the border between the dream of being a boy and the certainty of being a girl. With her brothers she accepts her femininity, even at the cost of being ridiculed, because it is quite natural for each sex to think that it is the best. Furthermore, Wendy, like her brothers, is very surprised when Peter praises the female sex.

Does he want to be a girl himself? A sad child needs to believe in the possibility of being boy and girl, man and woman. Wendy, on the other hand, is very fond of playing the little mother. This enables her to imitate her mother (for Peter Pan, however, there's never any question of being a father!), and it is certain that this voyage to Neverland is helping to prepare her for the future.

Yet she does not forget her true parents, and makes an effort to keep their memory alive for her brothers by telling stories about the family in London.

I believe that these tangible and true elements of her identity enable her to recognise the moment of danger when Neverland threatens to enclose upon them. She has the time to decide when to return to reality. She will doubtless always feel a tinge of nostalgia for Peter, but this will not prevent her from growing up and from having a child. The only unknown factor in all this is her husband, about whom nothing is written. In any case, we only have the author's word for this.

# CHAPTER 4

# Forgotten childhood

People who meet Peter Pan usually recognise the small child inside themselves, the one they tend to forget. Childhood memories are like that; one almost wonders whether they ever really existed. We're talking here of very early memories, like that of birth, or of having been held in one's mother's arms, or of having suckled at her breast. Then there is the memory of the time when she went away, leaving us alone, small and defenceless, screaming with despair because we did not know that she would come back.

We all share these experiences, but having grown up we thrust them into the background and are ashamed to think or talk about them. No one is likely to say, for example, even in the most intimate conversation: 'I remember how I slid along the tunnel, and how strange and frightening it was to come out of the warm sticky egg that was my mother's belly.'

Nobody talks that way! Or they speak about it differently; one dreams about passing through a channel and coming out the other side to avoid the risk of being smothered. Then one wakes up sweating, panting with fear! But it was just a dream.

When a mother brings her baby into the world (an exceptional moment in the life of a woman who, having sheltered another human being for nine months and having shared everything with it, will now let it emerge at the cost of an intense, volcanic, experience) she is reminded for a brief instant of her own birth. But the next minute, people are taking photographs of the baby, followed by the round of baptisms or circumcisions and, once again, it is as if nothing has happened.

These oversights are strange. Another important subject that no one talks about easily is the way in which the baby enters its mother's belly and in what form. It is extremely difficult for the children to picture themselves, and yet it is crucial for them to know their origins, and whether there was desire in their creation.

Then comes the day of parting, when we must leave our loved ones. This too is unimaginable. The death of a loved one is inconceivable; we are convinced that we shall exist forever. 'It is very sad that life is like a game of chess,' wrote Freud, 'a false move can force us to give up the game, with the difference that we cannot begin a second time.'

Thus, we forget these simple and obvious things; we do not talk about them, but they torment us from the beginning to the end of our existence.

## Archaeologists of the mind

For some people unravelling these questions is the very purpose of life. Like archaeologists they dedicate their time to exploring the mind's pre-historical caverns in the effort to retrieve those powerful moments that are otherwise so quickly forgotten. One of these archaeologists was Sigmund Freud; another was James Matthew Barrie, the author of Peter Pan.

It may seem peculiar to consider these two men together, one a Jew from Galicia who immigrated to Vienna, the other a Scotsman, a Protestant, who immigrated to London. They were born a few years apart, Sigmund Freud on 6 May 1856 in Freiberg, Moravia, and James Barrie four years and three days later, on 9 May 1860 in Kirriemuir, Scotland.

In my opinion both these men delved into their personal despair to construct a masterwork thanks to their lost childhood. No doubt they had other points in common. Both came from large families.

Freud was born in a modest house in Freiberg. He was the eldest son of Amalia, twenty years younger than her husband. His father already had two sons; one married with two children (the second had just been born) and the other one a bachelor, about Amalia's age. As a cloth merchant, he was not rich, but he had great ambitions for his son. Furthermore, Amalia consulted a fortune-teller who predicted that Sigmund would be a great man. Very early in his life he felt he was his mother's favourite, and this impression never left him:

> In my heart of hearts, deep down, the happy child of Freiberg always exists, the first-born of a young mother, nourished with these initial, indelible impressions, shaped by the soil of his birth.

Later, when he wrote about himself as a young man, he recognised the role of his mother's unconditional love in developing his triumphant self-esteem that led to his future success. Sigmund was eighteen months old when a second little boy, Julius, was born, who died seven months later. He never regretted the death of his rival:

> The child resents the undesired intruder, the rival. He reproaches him not only for nursing at his mother's breast, but also for any demonstration designed to attract maternal care. He feels himself dethroned, spoiled, and dispossessed of his rights. He harbours a jealous hatred for his little brothers and sisters, and develops resentment against his faithless mother, which he expresses by an unpleasant change in his behaviour. We rarely form a fair perception of the strength of these jealous impulses, of the tenacity with which they persist, and of their influence on our later development.

## A place to be taken

At the age of two-and-a-half, Freud suffered a genuine trauma with the birth of his sister Anna. Suddenly his mother disappeared from the house, and his half-brother Philip simultaneously dismissed a nurse who took care of him. The little boy desperately searched for the two women who counted most in his life. Philip explained that the nurse had been eingekästelt, 'put into a box' (a German expression which means imprisoned, because she was suspected of theft). Little Sigmund begged his brother to release his mother, the prisoner of the large chest sitting in his room. Had his mother also disappeared into a box?

When she reappeared, beautiful and slim, with the new rival, Sigmund asked whether it was not his brother Philip who had placed this baby inside his mother. This question, for the little two-and-a-half-year-old boy, was both crucial and dangerous.

It is the shadow of these original puzzles, instilled in the mind of the little Sigmund Freud, and forgotten for years, that probably sparked his passionate curiosity and wove the first fabric of psychoanalysis. So many mysteries for a child: his young mother pregnant with a rival; his big brother who seemed strangely implicated; his nephew, older than he, friend and enemy alike; his father who could have been his grandfather.

The disappearance of a mother, the birth of a baby, and the death of a father, can disorganise everything for a child and make him lose the sense of security that he first enjoyed. To recover his position, he is therefore tempted to take the place of his parents. Wendy, for instance, dethroned her mother in Neverland.

Children are not only clever, but they lie in wait for any opportunity to take the place of adults; the least confusion, the slightest flaw or shortcoming, can encourage them to seize power. This gives them the illusion of an advantage over the adult, or at least of occupying a position of strength.

Throughout his life, Freud retained a passionate attachment to his mother. In his theory, he particularly idealised the relationship between mother and son. In his eyes, every intimate and durable relationship is always tinted with ambivalence; in other words, love and hate intermingle at some time or other. The only relationship exempt from these contradictory feelings is the one between a mother and her son, because a relationship based on narcissism is not upset by rivalries.

Freud had unconditional faith in his relationship with his mother, and he never questioned it, even during his long years of self-analysis. He could never imagine that this love was diminished in any way by the affection his mother felt for her other children. Despite their presence, he knew he was the favourite.

Judaism, poverty, the ambitions that his parents had for him, and a milieu rich in primal fantasies, doubtless contributed significantly to the heroic courage with which he devoted himself to a difficult and original life's work.

## The wonderful boy

James Matthew Barrie was the ninth child and third son of a family of modest Scottish weavers. Like Freud, he was born in a very small house; everyone lived, slept, and ate in two rooms. The family was poor but full of ambition for the children.

David Barrie and Margaret Ogilvy's children, particularly the boys, were destined for study. David Barrie was a quiet man, highly respected in the small closed community of Kirriemuir. He was a weaver by profession and very intent on the education of his children. Margaret Ogilvy was a strong woman, self-taught in her own way, who had lost her mother when she was eight years old. She had the role of 'little mother' for her younger brother David, and housekeeper for her father.

James was the second last child to be born into the large family and was not particularly celebrated at his birth. The eldest son, Alexander, was already at the university, and his mother trusted him from the day he was born. But it was the second son, David, on whom Margaret concentrated all her ambitions and all her secret dreams. He was her favourite. Studious, calm, and handsome, there was not a doubt that he was destined for a brilliant career as a Protestant Minister, the highest ambition for a mother who had been a member of the 'Auld Licht' (a fundamentalist branch of Scottish Protestantism).

The young David espoused the wishes of his mother; he particularly shone in theology, and it was decided that he would continue his studies in the school where his brother Alexander taught. The pride she felt whenever he achieved good marks helped Margaret to bear his absence.

The winter of 1867 was extremely severe, and the small lake in front of the school in Bothwell froze over sufficiently for amateurs to skate.

Alexander had given David a pair of skates, which he shared with a friend. On the evening of David's fourteenth birthday, the children went skating on the lake. When David's friend took his turn, he shot off with all the strength of adolescence, and struck David, who fell headfirst onto the ice and fractured his skull. There was little hope of saving him, and Alexander sent his parents a telegram to break the bad news. This drama was to mark little James throughout his life. He wrote in *Margaret Ogilvy*, a book devoted to his mother:

> She had a son who was far away at school. I remember very little about him, only that he was a merry-faced boy who ran like a squirrel up a tree and shook the cherries into my lap. When he was thirteen, and I was half his age the terrible news came, and I have been told that the face of my mother was awful in its calmness as she set off to get between death and her boy. We trooped with her down the brae to the wooden station, and I think I envied her the journey in the mysterious wagons; I know we played around her, proud of our right to be there, but I do not recall it; I only speak from hearsay. Her ticket was taken, she had bidden us goodbye with that fighting face which I cannot see, and then my father came out of the telegraph office and said huskily, 'He's gone!' Then we turned very quietly and went home again up the brae.

## The beginning of the story

One day, his older sister, finding him sitting in front of his mother's closed door, unable to console him advised him to tell their mother that she still had another son!

> I went in excitedly, but the room was dark, and when I heard the door shut and no sound come from the bed, I was afraid, and I stood still. I suppose I was breathing hard, or perhaps I was crying, for after a time I heard a listless voice that had never been listless before say 'Is that you?' I think the tone hurt me for I made no answer, and then the voice said more anxiously 'Is that you?' again. I thought it was the dead boy she was speaking to and I said in a little lonely voice, 'No, it's not him, it's just me.' Then I heard a

cry, and my mother turned in bed, and though it was dark I knew that she was holding out her arms.

James never left his mother from that day on, trying by all possible means to take the place of his dead brother. He was caught between a dead brother and a little sister who was born three years after his birth. When little Julius disappeared, Sigmund Freud triumphed in his place as the favourite son. In the same way, when David disappeared, James took the place of the adored son. The two mothers in deep depression; two veiled maternal glances; two lost mothers mourning a little child.

At what moment did the story of James Matthew Barrie begin? Did his destiny begin at his birth, or was it at the age of six years when his mother locked herself into mourning for her favourite son? In *Margaret Ogilvy* he tells how his life seemed to be plunged into a thick fog for six years:

> It was all guess work for six years, and she whom I see in them is the woman who came suddenly into view when they were at an end. Her timid lips I have said, but they were not timid then, and when I knew her the timid lips had come. The soft face, they say, was not so soft then. In her happiest moments and never was a happier woman, her mouth did not of a sudden begin to twitch, and tears to lie on the mute blue eyes in which I have read all I know and would ever care to write. Those eyes that I cannot see until I was six years old have guided me through life, and I pray God they may remain my only earthly judge to the last.

What transpired between the lost mother and the son who remained so faithful? Volumes have been written about the life of James Matthew Barrie, the little man who was strangely full of mirth and yet at the same time so sad. Many authors have been interested in his literary and theatrical career and his tragic personal life.

The days and months spent on his mother's bed listening to her talk about his dead brother brought James Matthew to realise that she derived some comfort from the fact that David, dead so young, would remain a child forever.

## Magenta apron

'The child forever' became the source of inspiration for young James Barrie. When he was not playing the role of his dead brother, he invented a large number of characters whom he enjoyed staging in the laundry behind his house. He sometimes played the role of other boys:

> One day one of my friends came to see me, very sad because he was not allowed to play lest he damage the 'mourning blacks' in which he was attired. So, I nobly exchanged clothing with him for an hour, and in mine he disported forgetfully while I sat on a stone in his and lamented with tears, though I knew not for whom.

Throughout his childhood, Barrie developed an extraordinary capacity and 'a devouring desire to wear the feelings of others as if they were clothes'. He ceaselessly questioned his mother about her childhood:

> Those innumerable talks with her made her youth as vivid to me as my own, and so much more quaint, for, to a child, the oddest of things, and the most richly coloured picture book is that his mother was once a child also.

The 'childhood' of his mother and, so to speak, the 'child' in his mother was to be Barrie's main inspiration from the beginning of his life until the end. The story of the little orphan in her 'magenta apron' runs through his work in many forms: She was eight when her mother's death made her mistress of the house and mother to her little brother, and from that time she scrubbed and mended and baked and sewed—then she leapt outside, rushing out in a fit of childishness jumping, running to play hide and seek with children of her age.

These maternal tales occupied a large part of James's time. They gradually took form in his imagination and prepared the little mother Wendy in *Peter Pan*, the orphan of the Painted Lady in *Tommy and Grizel*, and many others.

> I soon grow tired of writing tales unless I can see a little girl, of whom my mother has told me, wandering confidently through the

pages. Such a grip has her memory of her girlhood upon me since I was a boy of six.

His father, David Barrie, is strangely absent. Barrie refers to him in passing in *Margaret Ogilvy* as 'a man I'm very proud to call my father'. In *Sentimental Tommy*, the father dies young and Tommy discovers his clothes folded on the chair. He has already forgotten the person who had worn these clothes.

## The blood of writing

James read many adventure books, with his mother; for example, *Robinson Crusoe, Tales of the Arabian Night*, and *Treasure Island*. He borrowed them from the library at the price of one penny for three days. He also subscribed to the Penny Dreadfuls, illustrated stories filled with tales of adventure, pirates of deserted islands, with blood and thunder on every page. One story also mentioned a little girl who sold watercress:

> This romantic little creature took such hold of my imagination that I cannot eat watercress even now without emotion. I lay in bed wondering what she would be up to in the next number. I know not whether it was owing to her loitering on the way for one month, to an extent that flesh and blood could not bear, or because we had exhausted the penny library, but on a day I conceived a glorious idea, or it was put into my head by my mother, then desirous of making progress with her new knitted hearthrug. The notion was nothing short of this; why should I not write the tales myself? I did write them—in the garret—but they by no means helped her to get on with her work, for when I finished a chapter I bounded downstairs to read it to her, and so short were the chapters, so ready was the pen that I was back with the new manuscript before another piece had been added to the rug … They were tales of adventure, (happy is he who writes adventures) no characters were allowed in if I knew their like in flesh and blood, the scene lay in unknown parts, desert islands, enchanted gardens, with knights on black chargers and round the first corner

a lady selling watercress. From the day on which I first tasted the blood of writing in the garret my mind was made up; there could be no boring profession for me; literature was my game.

The idea that he would have to grow up one day and abandon childhood games was unbearable to little James. For him, the end of childhood meant the end of everything: 'Nothing that happens to us after the age of twelve is worth much.'

Yet the five years he spent at the Dumfries Academy were filled with happiness. It was at Dumfries that he wrote his first play, *Bandelero the Bandit*, which was judged 'immoral' by the pastor, and which gave him some notoriety at the school.

At the age of seventeen, Barrie stopped growing, just short of 5 feet 4 inches (1.6 m). Completely beardless, he still lived like a very young boy. But he was not the only one; his friend, James Macmillan, from whom he was inseparable, was also thin and frail, 'a boy with a frightened look, poorly dressed and fragile'. Like David, he 'remained a boy forever', having died young.

The two friends took long walks, and talked of poetry, heroism, battles, and of the dead things that are said to escape only to return to earth during the terrible hour when night crosses paths with day:

> One day we wrote something about ourselves in cryptogram and hid it in a crevice in the ruin, agreeing to have another look for it when we were men. So when I was a man, I dug for it and found it, having then quite forgotten what it said. But before putting it back I spelt it out. It gave our names and ages, and said that Macmillan and I had begun to write a story of school life, 'by Didymuss' … School life is not what a boy usually takes as the subject of his first book, and I think there was something rather pathetic in the choice. It was as if we knew already that the next best thing to being boys is to write about them.

## The construction of Neverland

What is the true story of a life? If we ask an old person to relate his life, he replies, 'Oh, it was so long ago, I have forgotten …' He talks about his childhood, naturally. He remembers certain moments and spontaneously offers a bit of history: 'Oh, yes, I remember, when your mother was young and I …' Sometimes old images arise, and then … tears. Yet he is capable of not crying while evoking terrible tragedies, like the death of a son. Emotion seems absent; emptied of its substance like a corpse … or perhaps it is buried somewhere in a lapse of memory? But these gaps are not empty; the archaeologists of the mind can draw their content into the daylight, if only for a brief moment, just enough to recover the continuous thread of a story.

Like the circulation of blood in the body, psychic continuity ensures the life of the mind. When one comes to consult an archaeologist of the psyche, a 'soul digger', it is to divulge the splits, the failings in one's life, those that break the thread. Will the archaeologist tell us what this means?

Some lives are constructed like a patchwork: two bits are sewn together here, there a cheerful piece of brightly coloured fabric hides a hole … Sigmund Freud was deeply interested in these holes, and in the slips and oversights stuffed in the bottom. These enabled him to understand what was wrong with someone. When it becomes possible to reconstruct what has been forgotten, the true thread of the story emerges. The problem lies in finding out where the thread begins.

For example, when Peter Pan was still a baby in Kensington Gardens, we discovered that the true thread of a story lies in the strange confusion of feelings that assail us when we begin to live, to feel, but we cannot yet 'express' it. At the time, Peter believed that he was still a bird.

For Freud, the beginning of life is marked by 'great sensual pleasure' with the mother. If she is well, and has accepted being a mother, she can help her baby maintain the illusion that he can 'have and be everything'. This is her way of reassuring him and compensating for the shock suffered in leaving the comfortable and warm home, which was her belly.

To attenuate the painful passage and the loss of paradise, the baby becomes very active in the quest for this illusion. But the great sensual pleasure of the beginning, these feelings of grandeur, are doomed to disappear because the expectations, which they mask, are incompatible with reality. It is impossible to 'have and be everything'. For example, a small boy cannot become the husband of his mother, nor a little girl the wife of her father. Yet this desire emerges at some time or other in every child.

The unconscious repression of this illusion can bring about considerable distress, and endless moral suffering. The sensation of lost love and the ensuing impression of failure deeply wound one's self-esteem and procure feelings of inferiority. Later on in life, the loss of a loved one will often unconsciously reopen this early wound.

## Dangerous gamble

The first great challenge in the life of a little child is the spectre of the 'reality principle', that is of having to renounce immediate gratification to be able to grow up. Peter Pan rejected it deliberately and others do the same unconsciously.

The ability to relinquish great pleasure often depends on how much time the child had to enjoy this with his mother. If this period was not long enough or if there was a sudden break in continuity, the child will be tempted to prolong the spell artificially in order to retain the illusion of being 'everything'. He will become Peter Pan!

It can occur that the unconscious aim of an entire life is to recover this paradise lost or never known. For instance, a man, who had been abandoned by his parents as a small child, sought help because he could not stop searching for the lost sensations of his childhood. For him, the quest became so urgent that he left his wife and family to live with another couple and their children for many years, with the sole aim of retrieving these moments of early happiness that he experienced from time to time.

Thereby Neverland serves as a hole to be filled with lost objects, which the child is incapable of giving up. All these bits and pieces exude an air of 'family', because they tend to include those of the parents, as if nostalgia were transmitted from mother to daughter, from father to son.

Sometimes the most precious 'treasure' that parents bestow on their children is the 'malaise', which they themselves have suffered. It is as if they were desperate to share their pain. A young woman was tormented by the fact that her mother did not love her father, and betrayed him with another man. When it was her turn to find a companion, she picked a man with whom strife would be guaranteed: far removed from her own culture and her deepest needs. The inevitable repetition ensued: their union was filled with violence and suffering, and the children in turn witnessed the infidelities that had distressed their mother's childhood.

Barrie's mother had lost her own mother at the age of eight. Little Jamie lost his mother at age six, in a manner that was undoubtedly much worse than if she had actually died.

When a young child loses his childhood, and his life is disorganised, he is forced to find a solution. Faced with such a catastrophic situation his personal strategy will be to return to the past, to recover those 'all-powerful feelings' when he was master of his world.

Shortly after my father died, I discovered the solution for maintaining the 'great pleasure'. I began by absorbing my father's role. Not a light task for an eleven-year-old girl! I deliberately overlooked my own development and became very responsible, indeed too responsible. Since I concentrated on finding solutions to ensure my mother's well-being, I had no time left for the necessary work of 'growing up' and leaving my childhood toys behind. I clung all the more fiercely to objects of the past, the treasures of my early years, the rabbit that remained imprisoned behind the barbed wires surrounding Hungary.

## Monuments to dead children

Neverland is bursting with a multitude of past pleasures, which can no longer be satisfactorily experienced in the present. These relics from the past become museum pieces, beautiful and fragile. If we succeed in identifying this sacred tabernacle in the prehistory of an individual and transform these ancient objects, affording them a new life, we can begin to create a real story in the present. Yet the opening of this intimate and secret place is a terribly painful undertaking, and few dare venture therein.

Freud observed that writers have a great deal to teach us about these buried treasures.

> Writers of fiction are most valuable allies and their work is to be prized highly, for they know much more of a whole host

of things between heaven and earth of which our philosophy cannot even dream.

In his study of the *Gradiva*, a work of fiction by Jensen, he describes a certain form of forgetting, recognisable by the force with which it buries memory, despite a very powerful pull to emerge. It is as if an interior resistance fought its reappearance. Nevertheless, such forgotten memories conserve a considerable active capacity that can be revived under the influence of an external event. But the psychic consequences resulting from a modification of the forgotten souvenir often remain incomprehensible to the subject.

'You may drive out nature with a pitchfork, but she will always return,' Freud declared, and the violence of this return depends on the strength with which it has been prevented. Gradiva relates the story of a young man who refused to love a woman and fell desperately in love with a Roman statue:

> The arousal of the repressed eroticism came precisely from the field of the instruments that served to bring about the repression. It was appropriate that an antique, marble sculpture of a woman be the object that tore our archaeologist away from his refusal of love and reminded him of his obligation to pay the debt to life with which we are encumbered from our birth.

So, what is the true story of James Matthew Barrie? Is it the story that others have written about him? The story he wrote about himself? The story of Peter Pan? Freud believed that, in the world of fiction, novelistic or theatrical, we try to retrieve what we have lost in life. In this case, Peter Pan holds the essential key that might open Neverland created by James Matthew Barrie. After all, didn't Barrie himself claim that he no longer remembered having written the story of Peter Pan? The secret, as we have seen, hides in the forgotten hollows of the mind.

## The right keys

Peter had lost his mother, but in fact it was he who left to play with the fairies. When he was ready to return, the window was barred, and another child was sleeping in his bed!

James Barrie never left his mother after the death of his brother David. Perhaps, among his forgotten memories, he hid the sensation of having stolen her from the dead brother. Who knows, perhaps for a moment he played with the thought that it was he who had killed him to finally possess the desired mother.

When someone visits an archaeologist seeking aid to dig into the caves of the mind, the key to secrets from the past are often present at the very first meeting. If the archaeologist is skilful, he stores these in the corner of his memory and produces them only when the person is ready to recognise and make use of them. It is inept showing them at a time when the patient is not yet ready to comprehend their value. Sometimes archaeologists, especially newcomers to the profession, are tempted to reveal their talent in disclosing the keys. It is absolutely essential to avoid this 'showing off' as it can have costly effects for both archaeologist and the patient.

The first pages of *Margaret Ogilvy* resemble one of these initial encounters; the keys to Neverland are quickly detected:

> On the day I was born we bought six hair-bottomed chairs, and in our little house it was an event, the first great victory in a woman's long campaign; how they had been laboured for, the pound-note and the thirty-three penny-bits they cost, what anxiety there was about the purchase, the show they made in possession of the west room, my father's unnatural coolness when he brought them in (but his face was white)—I so often heard the tale afterwards, and shared as boy and man in so many similar triumphs, that the coming of the chairs seems to be something I remember, as if I had jumped out of bed on that first day, and run ben to see how they looked.

> I am sure my mother's feet 'were ettling to be ben long' before they could be trusted, and that the moment after she was left alone with me she was discovered barefooted in the west room, doctoring a scar (which she had been the first to detect) on one of the chairs, or sitting on them regally, or withdrawing and re-opening the door suddenly to take the six by surprise. And then, I think, a shawl was flung over her (it is strange to me to think it was not I who ran after her with the shawl), and she

was escorted sternly back to bed and reminded that she had promised not to budge … Thus was one little bit of her revealed to me at once: I wonder if I took note of it.

It seems that little Jamie hardly had the time to be born when his mother's gaze was already turned towards 'the hair-bottomed chairs' that were so important for herself and the family! 'A great victory for this woman.' No sooner was she left alone with him than she went off to look at her chairs—he would have loved to have accompanied her to cover her with her shawl; it was inconceivable that there was a time when it was not he who covered her. It was unimaginable to have been a baby. Had his mother forgotten to weigh him at his birth? Yet this scene appeared to him to be so real he wondered whether he had not already made notes on the subject.

The neighbours came to see the little boy and the chairs (as if both were of the same value). Naturally, Margaret agreed with them, the child would never go to university; after all, they were just like them, in the same condition, naturally, naturally … But in these words, spoken over his cradle, did the baby Jamie already detect the secret wishes of his mother, the burning ambitions behind the dear face? Because the chairs were only the beginning:

> And when we were left together, did I laugh at the great things that were in her mind, or had she to whisper them to me first, and then did I put my arm around her and tell her that I would help? Thus it was for such a long time: it is strange to me to feel that it was not so from the beginning.

One may remember that Peter Pan had flown off to the fairies on the day he was born, when he had heard his parents planning his future.

Jamie seemed to have emerged from his mother's womb to enter her dreams of grandeur immediately. He was very attentive to maternal desire, to the point where he wanted to go and see the chairs with her, instead of telling her: 'Well, mother, I've arrived, it is I that you must look at, because, if you don't, I won't be able to love myself!'

Jamie's life began with Margaret's gaze diverted to inanimate objects, to chairs, which decorated the main room of the house.

Poor Jamie! It was the very beginning of Neverland—the gaze of the mother, dearly desired but not obtained, an endless search in every woman's gaze—a mother.

## The victim of tragedy

Wendy knew that not having a mother was a tragedy; Peter simply had no idea what the word meant. This often happens with persons who have experienced trauma but feel nothing. The emotions and passions survive the event and explode unexpectedly. For example, one sees persons sobbing uncontrollably at the cinema, crying alone among a tearless crowd. Although feelings have been separated from the event, they remain intact.

For little Jamie, his mother's diverted gaze was a tragedy. We can picture him, like the baby Peter Pan carried naked into the icy Kensington Gardens, deprived of the vital warmth of the maternal fabric. In fact, he tried to compensate for her lack of warmth by inventing a  fantasy:  on the day of his birth, he covered her with a shawl to protect her from the cold. Had he already renounced becoming a fully-fledged human being, having decided on the day of his birth to sacrifice himself for the fragile, ambitious mother with the distracted gaze? Had he agreed to remain a 'half-and-half', one part for himself, and another for his mother; was he aware of this choice? Or had he forgotten the tragedy, and remained 'gay, innocent, and heartless'?

Solomon had predicted that Peter would remain a 'betwixt-and-between'. Jamie gave himself to his mother like the tragic little goat, sacrificed in ancient times during the feasts of Dionysus: half-god, the god Pan, and half devil, the god of lust and putrefaction … At the end of *Peter Pan in Kensington Gardens*, a little girl comes to give Peter a goat to keep him company. A goat for a child, a child as a goat, Barrie's childhood sacrificed to Margaret Ogilvy, his mournful mother.

The evidence of this tragedy are the powerful emotions and feelings that his writing evokes in the reader. Like the archaeologist who reconstructs history through the vestiges and objects uncovered by his excavations, the archaeologist of the mind works with words, disclosing the feelings that they mask, in the search for their hidden meaning:

> Peter called, 'Mother! Mother!' but she heard him not; in vain he beat his little limbs against the iron bars. He had to fly back, sobbing, to the gardens, and he never saw his dear again. What a glorious boy he had meant to be to her! Ah, Peter! We who have made the great mistake, how differently we should all act at the second chance. But Solomon was right—there is no second chance, not for most of us. When we reach the window, it is Lock-out Time. The iron bars are up for life.

Did James Barrie think he had his second chance the day when, in his mother's room, as she was mourning the death of her favourite son, he cried: 'No, mother, it's only me,' and she stretched out her arms to him with a sob?

Like Peter, who found his place in a thrush's nest, Barrie finally found a niche in his mother's mind, in her Neverland, where the dead children are immortalised. Could he have done otherwise? Was this the only place for him? In any case, once installed, he never left it. Yet he tried to save the half of himself he still possessed: to survive, he began to write. The wandering child, the lost boys, a little girl who becomes mother, Peter Pan, the little white bird: all James Barrie's characters are proof of that deep emotion that clung to him like the christening robe. The robe came to symbolise the lost child searching for his mother from the day he was born and never able to separate from her without losing himself.

## The child doctor

James Matthew Barrie's second chance was writing. His novels captured 'the little girl in her magenta apron' and never let her go. Perhaps in this way he retained the means of becoming 'the wonderful boy he had wanted to be for her', and one of the 'halves' of him clung passionately to this project. The assurance that she could love the prodigal child gave him hope of ultimately loving himself. Yet he had a second plan, much more altruistic, to cure his mother and to make her laugh:

> After that I sat a great deal in her bed trying to make her forget him, which was my crafty way of playing physician, and if I saw any one out of doors do something that made the others laugh, I immediately hastened to that dark room and did it before her. I suppose I was an odd little figure; I have been told that my anxiety to brighten her gave my face a strained look and put a tremor into the joke (I would stand on my head in the bed, my feet against the wall, and then cry excitedly, 'Are you laughing, mother?') and perhaps what made her laugh was something I was unconscious of, but she did laugh suddenly now and then, whereupon I screamed exultantly to that dear sister, who was ever in waiting, to come and see the sight, but by the time she came the soft face was wet again. Thus I was deprived of some of my glory, and I remember once only making her laugh before witnesses. I kept a record of her laughs on a piece of paper, a stroke for each, and it was my custom to show this proudly to the doctor every morning.

Little Jamie tried so assiduously to comfort his mother that other members of the family, particularly his sister Jane Ann, Margaret Ogilvy's favourite daughter, actively encouraged him in his task. Jane Ann one day suggested that he speak about the dead child to his mother:

> I did not see how this could make her the merry mother she used to be, but I was told that if I could not do it nobody could, and this made me eager to begin. At first, they say I was often jealous, stopping her fond memories with the cry, 'Do you mind nothing about me?' but that did not last; its place was taken by an intense desire (again, I think, my sister must have breathed it into life) to become so like him that even my mother should not see the I difference, and many and artful were the questions I put to that end.

Jamie thus set about rummaging in his mother's memory to learn David's gestures and behaviour down to the tiniest detail. This game soon became a genuine task for the child. He applied himself with the zeal that a good actor enlists in preparing his role, as if his life depended on it.

In the same way, Peter Pan in Kensington Gardens 'played at playing' like a real child, but the real child remained David, and Jamie was nothing but a false David, an intruder.

One day he felt ready: wearing his brother's clothes, he took up David's typical stance in front of his mother, legs akimbo, hands in his pockets, head held high: the posture of Peter Pan!

> I stood still until she saw me, and then how it must have hurt her! 'Listen!' I cried in a glow of triumph, and I stretched my legs wide apart and plunged my hands into the pockets of my knickerbockers, and began to whistle.

The gesture of this tragic little goat who sacrifices his life to seduce his mother, giving her both pain and pleasure, marks the birth of Peter Pan!

Jamie becomes David, Jamie becomes Peter Pan, Peter Pan is David and Jamie plays at being the dead child.

Peter returned to his sleeping mother's bedside, but she looked sad, and he knew why she looked sad. One of her arms moved as if it wanted to go round something, and he knew what it wanted to go round. He also knew that he held the secret of his mother's happiness and, without the shadow of a doubt, that he was capable of giving her the greatest gift that a woman can receive, a little boy of her own!

All little boys dream one day or another of being able to give their mother a baby, but they give up the idea because they realise that this must be the father's privilege. One wonders if the notion of 'father' even existed for Peter Pan.

## The finest gift

Jamie gave the gift of the 'wonderful little boy' to his mother: it was himself. But, if the truth were known, he was actually of two minds: 'Sometimes he looked longingly at his mother, and sometimes he looked longingly at the window …'

To be Jamie meant accepting a 'dead' mother mourning for a dead child. Jamie wanted to be her 'wonderful boy', her David! Again, in other words David meant undertaking an endless adventure, acquiring the illusion that he could be his mother's favourite and to exist at the age of six. Yet for this, as for everything else, there was a price to pay: he was going to have wings, but he would never quite be himself again.

Jamie, entering the room, discovered his mother lying in her bed (note the absence of a father barring his way). Peter wanted to please his slumbering mother: 'It would have been pleasant to hear her cries of joy when she would clasp him in her arms, and, above all, how delicious that would be for her!'

However, such a great pleasure offered to a grown woman like his mother can also frighten a little boy. Was it this fear that told Peter not to wake her up? He hesitated to call 'Mother,' as he refrained from kissing her, for fear that 'the joy of the kiss' would wake her. He finally found a solution: 'He played her a lovely kiss on his pipe, he never stopped playing until she looked happy and then he flew back to the Gardens'—just as Jamie decided to play for his mother to make her laugh.

It is not possible to hate a sad mother who cries. Yet the child needs to be angry with his mother to prove that she can survive his blows and his hatred. A mother's resistance certifies his own existence because he too will survive the storm unscathed.

But a sad mother is liable to succumb to such an attack. The sad child is not free to test his mother's strength; he must protect her from everything, even from his own hateful impulses. The fear that she could disappear at any moment keeps him in a fragile state that prevents him from expressing his own desire. Love and hate remain separate and assume a disproportionate scale, because proof of survival is impossible to obtain. Every feeling becomes dangerous, even murderous.

So the child remains torn 'between two desires'; he wants to have his mother entirely to himself, as in the beginning, and at the same time she frightens him. We noted Freud's belief that every human being is 'between two desires', except the son for his mother. Love between son and mother is untarnished and not ambivalent. Did Freud carry this into his theory in order to protect his mother? He too wanted to be the 'wonderful boy', and was nostalgic for the good old days.

Barrie declared that he could not remember having existed before the age of six. He knew that the 'timid lips' and the 'gentle face' of his mother had not always been so, as if they could have masked the terrible mother who frightened the little boys at night, as she appeared in their dreams. How to admit one's fear of a mother whose gaze is veiled by tears? How to hate this deeply wounded woman? For James Barrie and for Freud, only an ardent desire was possible for such a special mother!

## The bridal veil

Yet she clearly assumed another form at night. Let us remember: Peter Pan was often very agitated at night, and Wendy had to take him in her arms to calm him down. Barrie writes:

> When this horrid nightmare got hold of me, and how, I cannot say, but it has made me the most unfortunate of men. In my early boyhood it was a sheet that tried to choke me in the night. At school it was my awful bedfellow with whom I wrestled nightly while all the other boys in the dormitory slept with their consciences at rest. It had assumed shape at that time: leering, but fatally fascinating; it was never the same, yet always recognizable. One of the horrors of my dream was that I knew how it would come each time, and from where. I do not recall it in my childhood, but they tell me that, asleep in my cot, I would fling my arms about wildly as if fighting a ghost. It would thus seem that my nightmare was with me even then, though perhaps only as a shapeless mass that a too lively imagination was soon to resolve into a woman beautiful and cruel, with a bridal veil over her face. When I see her, she is still a long way off, but she approaches rapidly. I cower in a corner till she glides into the room and beckons me to follow her … Her power is mesmeric, for when she beckons, I rise and follow her, shivering, but obedient. We seem to sail as the crow flies to the church which I attended as a child, and there everyone is waiting for us …

One hideous night she came for me in a cart. I was seized hold of by invisible hands and flung into it. A horrible fear possessed me that I was being taken away to be hanged, and struggled to escape … My hands were bound together with iron chains, and as soon as I snapped them a little boy with wings forged another pair. Many a time when awake I have seen pictures of that little boy generally with arrows in his hands, one of which he is firing at some man or woman. In pictures he looks like a cherub who has over-eaten himself, but, ah, how terribly disfigured he is in my dreams! He is lean and haggard now, grown out of his clothes, and a very spirit of malignity. She drives the cart, laughing horribly as we draw nearer and nearer the church, while he sits behind me and occasionally jags me with an arrow. When I cry out in pain she turns and smiles upon him, and he laughs in gay response.

Can one possibly measure the colossal energy mobilised by this little boy to replace the dead child, to make his mother laugh, and to repair her wound at the risk of losing his identity?

The power and permanence of this nightmare exposes the pain of renunciation, at the price of his own sexuality. Obviously, however, he derived pleasure from suffering with his mother. We begin to understand how passionately he listened to Margaret's stories. With the voracity of a cannibal, he wanted to take everything from her, and control everything inside her (just as Peter Pan became dangerous when he desired Wendy's stories).

## Empty costume

Margaret Ogilvy's father, 'the only hero of her life', was a stonemason. A man worn out by a life of stone cutting, with a severe cough that swept him away nine months before Barrie's birth. Yet all the tales Margaret told Jamie about his grandfather immediately became real for the child, to the point where he describes them in the present:

It is a night of rain or snow, and my mother, the little girl in a pinafore who is already his housekeeper, has been many times to the door to look for him. At last he draws nigh, coughing …

Or he is in this chair reciting his favourite poem for her, The Cameronian's Dream and from the moment of the first lines, so solemnly uttered, 'In a dream of the night I was wafted away', she screams with excitement, just as I screamed long afterwards when she repeated these lines in his voice for me.

The sad child who has lost his childhood tries to capture the childhood of a parent, or of other children. I too listened tirelessly to the stories that my mother told me of her childhood: I visualised the huge garden in which she hid to eat apricots, while revelling in the adventures of *The Slave of the Huns* by Géza Gardony ... the big kitchen table around which the ten children took their meals with their parents ... The sunlit morning when grandmother chatted with her daughters for hours around coffee: 'Well, children, what shall we have for lunch today?' Then there were wonderful stories of Aunt Ethel who was married in Moscow to one of the Tsar's ministers. The gilded satins, the jewels, the bells of the Kremlin, the tinkling of the troika on the snow ... 'B-r-r-r-r!' cried Alyosha, bringing the horses to a halt. 'Njianichka daragaja!' exclaimed my cousins when they reached Hungary, fleeing the October Revolution! I didn't need novels; my head was full of my mother's stories, as if I had been there!

The death of a parent can plunge someone into Neverland. There everything is possible; for example, little girls can become mothers of their brothers and housekeepers for their fathers. Like Peter playing father to the lost boys, one plays at being an adult, the next minute returning to being a small child; being an adult is just a game.

One wonders who this grandfather was for little Jamie, his mother's unique hero, from whom he borrowed the cough that would later carry him off as well. Was this his adopted father? Of his real father he said nearly nothing. When he mentioned his parents' marriage, it was as if he spoke of a personal event. Once again, he is on the outside of his own childhood (we know that time does not exist in Neverland). On the other hand, an accurate description of the father is available in *Sentimental Tommy*; let us judge for ourselves:

Of this man who was his father he could get no hold. He could feel his presence, but never see him. Yet he had a face. It sometimes pressed Tommy's face against it in order to hurt him, which it could do, being all short needles at the chin … There came a time when the man was always in bed, but still Tommy could not see his face. What he did see was the man's clothes lying on the large chair just as he had placed them there when he undressed for the last time. The black coat and worsted waistcoat which he could take off together were on the seat, and the light trousers hung over the side, the legs on the hearthrug, with the red socks still sticking in them: a man without a body.

Who can rival a man without a body? Jamie's true rival was always David. He knew it when he looked at Margaret sleeping:

> … even while she slept her lips moved and she smiled as if he had come back to her [Peter Pan at the window] and when she woke, he might vanish so suddenly that she started up bewildered and looked about her, and then said slowly, 'My David's dead!' or perhaps he remained long enough to whisper why he must leave her now, and then she lay silent with filmy eyes.

It was difficult to hate David, a dead child. It is by writing that James Matthew Barrie avenged himself, bared his teeth, and bit whomever he wanted, including his mother. It is thus that he wrote a novella entitled *Dead for Twenty Years* about a similar tragedy in the life of another woman. It was the only story of which his mother never spoke to anyone.

How can one avoid feeling hostility towards a sad mother? A lost child, now a grown man, dreamt that his mother was a witch: 'I see a woman dressed in black. The scene is set on the seashore; the weather is icy; she wears a veil and dances around me singing: "You have no pupils, you have no pupils!"'

The little 'aviator', who for many years could draw nothing but aeroplanes, was obliged to stop seeing me. He knew from the beginning of our sessions that his mother could not tolerate his coming to see me for long. She withdrew him rapidly from anything he undertook (even if she had organised it for him). He protected her closely. He always worried about her. One day, we took out the plasticine, and I realised that he needed a knife to complete a major task. He started on the plasticine, tearing it, chopping it up, and cutting it … a real butchery! He then left, contented.

## The fierce joy of loving too much

There were other children in little Jamie's house, all those babies in whom Margaret laid her ambitions: 'I see her bending over the cradle of her first-born, college for him already in her eye.' There was a second daughter: was she Tinker Bell, the little fairy Tinker Bell ready to sacrifice her life for Peter Pan? 'From the first day on,' writes Barrie, 'the child followed my mother with the most wistful eyes, as if she guessed how much she needed help and longed to jump up and give it.'

Jane Ann clung to her mother's needs so intensely that she decided to care for her all her life, as if Margaret Ogilvy had assigned her the role of the mother whom she had lost at the age of eight. Jane Ann even managed to die before her mother by a few days. Her daily anguish, her pains were overlooked by all, including herself. When Barrie arrived from London, the two women were already dead.

> I saw my mother lying stretched out, her face beautiful and calm. But it was the other room I entered first, and it was by my sister's side that I fell upon my knees. The rounded completeness of a woman's life that was my mother's had not been for her. She would not have it at the price. 'I'll never leave you, mother.' 'Fine, I know you'll never leave me.' The fierce joy of loving too much, it is a terrible thing. My sister's mouth was firmly closed, as if she had got her way.

'The fierce joy of loving too much' recalls the earliest love when baby and mother are one, before 'the two desires', love and hate, arrive to confuse everything. These are the 'two desires' that complicate life; some people cannot admit that hatred and anger can spoil 'the fierce joy of loving too much'; they think that hatred can be set aside. Like the crocodile prowling around Captain Hook, hatred begins to live a separate life, strengthened, it attacks those who pretend to ignore it, and kills those it loves most, seducing them to an irresistible death.

Freud was intrigued by the lost child, shrouded in the shadow of a dead brother. The child feels hatred because this loss is violent, attacking him constantly. He fears that it will kill him. Self-sacrifice is often the culmination of this interior hatred.

In the midst of a fragile, mourning mother, shadowed by a dead mother, a tragic sister, a dead brother, and a bodiless father, Jamie could only fear his hatred and the presumed danger that it represented for his loved ones. Later on, many literary critics qualified his writings as 'sadistic'.

## Self-awareness

Rivalry, hatred and unspoken violence towards his loved ones found an outlet in Barrie's writing, as if to help him settle accounts. Peter Pan cuts off Captain Hook's arm; Hook bites Peter; the boys kill the pirates; Peter kills the boys that grow up; and the crocodile is always lurking, with the clock of death ticking away to remind us that every moment counts towards our final destiny.

But it is in *Sentimental Tommy* that Barrie describes the emotions and the disarray of his life without disguise. He makes us feel the deep despair of a young boy upon the birth of an 'intruder'; his little sister Maggie was born when little Jamie was only three years old. She usurped his place as the baby of the family, just as Freud had been 'replaced' by his little sister.

Tommy is seated on the stairs with his friend Shovel in a poor neighbourhood of London where he lives with his mother. The two children see the doctor coming to visit Tommy's mother: '"It's a kid or a coffin," he said sharply, knowing that only birth or death brought a doctor here.'

It soon becomes obvious that the imminent arrival of a baby is involved, and Tommy is convinced that he simply has to watch the staircase to prevent the intruder from passing through. We can imagine his disappointment when he finally returns home and his mother, exhausted, deep in her bed, calls him:

> She guessed that he had heard the news and stayed away
> through jealousy of his sister, and by and by she said, with a

faint smile: 'I have a present for you, laddie.' But when she went to show him the baby, he cringed, and cries out: 'No, no, keep her covered up!'

Just like Peter Pan, when Wendy wanted to turn up the light to show him that she had become a woman: 'For almost the only time in his life, that I know of, Peter was afraid. "Don't turn up the light," he cried.' Like the little aviator who came to see me, when we talked about the birth of babies: 'No, no, I don't want to know!'

Tommy, jealous, suddenly deprived of his mother's hands, cries: 'It's true what Shovel says, you don't love me never again; you jest loves that little limmer!' Like Jamie, who accused his mother: 'You only love David!'

'Nah, nah,' the mother answered, passionate at last, 'she can never be to me what you have been, my laddie, for you came to me when my home was in hell, and we held it together, you and me.'

## Choosing one's heroine

The complicity between a mother and her child, especially when it works against the father, is extremely damaging. It means the loss of childhood, sometimes the loss of life.

I learned one day about an adolescent boy who heard the cries of his mother in his parents' bedroom. Knowing that she was rejecting her husband's advances, he pushed open the door and struck his father. A few months later, he developed a lump in his throat that turned out to be throat cancer. He died shortly afterwards. The parents cursed their destiny, but no one worried about the boy's mental suffering. The boy was the only man who counted in his mother's life.

Day and night, love and hate, to know and not to know; the two desires become one. Jamie wanted to know, and at the same time did not want to know from whence babies came ('All babies, before being born, are birds').

We have learned that on the very day of his birth, it comforted him to think that he was already taking care of his mother. Perhaps he would simply have liked to arrive through the window like Peter Pan on that fatal night. To admit where babies really come from is to admit also that there is a father and a mother, as well as the desire they feel for each other. Jamie could not, did not want to accept this; his whole life depended on it, because his mother had to be his and his alone.

At the beginning of his writing career, he and his mother read in a newspaper that a good novelist must have a perfect knowledge of himself and of a woman close to him:

> My mother said, 'Know yourself, for everybody must know himself' (there never was a woman who knew less about herself than she), and she would add dolefully, 'But I doubt I'm the only woman you know well.' 'Then I must make you my heroine,' I said lightly. 'A gey auld-farrant-like heroine!' She said, and we both laughed at the notion so little did we read the future.

By taking his mother as a heroine, James Barrie declared to his mother, just as his sister had done: 'I shall never leave you.' At the end of the book *Margaret Ogilvy* he confirms this, his words the tragic weight of a son who has never been able to let go of his mother:

> And if I also live to a time when age must dim my mind and the past comes sweeping back like the shades of night over the bare road of the present it will not, I believe, be my youth I shall see but hers, not a boy clinging to his mother's skirt and crying, 'Wait till I'm a man, and you'll lie on feathers', but a little girl in a magenta frock and a white pinafore, who comes toward me through the long parks, singing to herself, and carrying her father's dinner in a flagon.

## The child who does not want to grow up

Barrie did not want to, and could not, let go of the image of the little girl who became a mother; all his heroines refer to it—Wendy, Grizel, Mary Rose, and Margaret Ogilvy:

> When it was known that I had begun another story my mother might ask what it was to be about this time. 'Fine, we can guess who it is about,' my sister would say pointedly.

Margaret would play innocent, and his sister would add that it was high time that he keeps her out of the books. Barrie adds that, as usual, his mother would give herself away unconsciously:

> 'That is what I tell him,' she says, chuckling, 'and he tries to keep me out, but he canna; it's more than he can do!'

Margaret Ogilvy was a perfect accomplice of the influence that she and her son exerted on each other. She perfectly understood that one might not want to grow up; she too had not been unable to live her childhood; her skirts had 'never been short', and her father had remained the only hero of her existence. To grow up, one must be able to let go of one's initial fantasies, one's heroes, and heroines of early childhood. Only then can one find another hero or heroine from a different family, with whom, despite everything, one wishes to spend one's life.

Did James Matthew Barrie know that his mother's hold on him would prevent him from loving a woman? There is a very poignant passage in *Tommy and Grizel*, when Grizel, knowing that Tommy has been finally released from the influence of his sister, comes to see him full of love and hope:

> Her arms made a slight gesture towards him, her hands were open, and she was giving herself to him. She could not see. For a fraction of time the space between them seemed to be annihilated. His arms were closing around her. 'Grizel!' He tried to be true to her by deceiving her; it was the only way. 'At last, Grizel,' he cried, 'at last!' and he put joyousness into his voice. 'It has all come right, dear one!' he cried like an ecstatic lover. Never in his life had he tried so hard to deceive at the sacrifice of himself. But he was fighting something as strong as the instinct of self-preservation, and his usually expressionless face gave the lie to his joyous words. Loud above his voice, his ashen face was speaking to her, and she cried in terror, 'What is wrong?' Even then he attempted to deceive her, but suddenly she guessed the truth. 'You don't want to be married!' 'I want to be married above all else on earth,' he said determinedly, but his face betrayed him still, and she demanded the truth, and he was forced at last to tell it.

A little shiver passed through her; that was all. 'Do you mean that you don't love me?' she said. 'You must tell me what you mean.'

'That is how others would put it, I suppose,' he replied. 'I believe they would be wrong. I think I love you in my own way, but I thought I loved you in their way, and it is the only way that counts in this world of theirs. It does not seem to be my world. I was given wings, I think, but I am never to know that I have left the earth until I come flop upon it, with an arrow through them. I crawl and wriggle here, and yet'—he laughed harshly—'I believe that I am a fine fellow when I am flying.'

Barrie is Peter Pan, full of gaiety flying through the air towards Neverland. If only he could find a Wendy to accompany him. But the image of the wing pierced by an arrow is specifically that of Wendy, wounded by the lost boys while approaching the island.

Even if he wanted to remain a 'little boy forever', it would be wrong to believe that Barrie was uninterested in girls, on the contrary. Yet he found that they did not pay him enough attention.

College was still a place of childhood, and the serious question of 'women' did not really arise. It was at Edinburgh University that he began to feel the solitude of a man who had remained a 'small boy' among men. This situation offered him the opportunity to watch the others, and to collect these observations as genuine treasures, like a scholar conducting research into beings from another planet. Just like Peter Pan, who spied on the real children so that he could learn to play like them. Barrie wrote in his notebook:

> Men can't get together without talking filth.
> He looks very young—trial of his life that he be taken for a boy.
> Far finer and nobler things in the world than loving a girl & possessing her
> Greatest horror: I dream that I am married—wake up shrieking.
> Growing up and giving up marbles … awful thought.

Poor little half-and-half! One feels from his notes the extent to which he remained on the outside of the life of ordinary humans! Just like Peter Pan in Kensington Gardens, he remained between two worlds. Even his writing was inspired by his mother's reminiscences and thoughts.

She wanted to inculcate noble and fine thoughts in the mind of her son. The sexual aspect of adult life was missing from her stories; these she considered as vulgar and dirty.

## Baptismal robe

Even if she didn't think much about men and women, Margaret Ogilvy certainly had babies and mothers in her head. She, who had lost her own mother at the age of eight, nurtured a true passion for little children from very early on, to the point of drawing dress patterns for hours on end, intended for her future offspring,

Babies and babies' robes were all that was left of her mother, the memory of the warmth of her body, the tenderness of her love. Who knows whether Peter Pan was not in fact the baby Margaret Ogilvy, who continued to mourn her departed mother?

Later, following the death of her son David, she reclaimed the robe in which all her children had been baptised and refused to part with it, as if the inanimate object represented more for her than her living child. Like the reminder of an absent love, but which surpasses all love:

'There was nothing in the house that spoke to her with more eloquence than the little white robe,' Barrie remembered. 'After all the children who had worn it, it had remained a baby forever.' In the hour of her death, Margaret again asked for the robe, and as soon as she had it in her hands, clasped it to herself, on her face, 'the mysterious fervour of motherhood'.

Was it motherhood or rather her own mother whom she found with her last breath? Like the babies who cling to a little piece of cloth that emanates the odour of their mother, was not Margaret seeking in the baby's robe the trace of her mother deceased too soon?

Is it possible to leave a dead mother? The essential passage between loving one's mother as a child and loving another human being as an adult is a very difficult one for all children. Is the sad child capable of making the transition? The 'passers' know how challenging it is for human beings to cross the border of childhood, withdrawing from parental destinies, in order to desire a person of the opposite sex.

Why are we all so caught up in our parents' lives? So determined by the words, often unsaid and even unknown, pronounced above our cradles? Upon leaving our mother's womb, it is just as if we hurried to cling to these desires, to reassure ourselves that we actually were human beings and not birds.

Those who have not been able to latch on to parental desires, abandoned babies, for example, often wonder whether they have not begotten themselves, without parental desire. But this is a terrible thought, because only monsters and some plants can engender themselves. Better to hang on to risky parental desires than to consider oneself a monster.

Yet when parental longings are too deeply buried in Neverland, they can take an unfavourable route, especially if the father or mother were himself or herself lost children. When parental plans are ignored or denied they can become a matter of life or death for the child. James Barrie must have suspected this because his Peter Pan flees to Kensington Gardens when he overhears his parents' plans. Unfortunately, Barrie was unable to apply this knowledge to his own destiny as he surrendered to his mother's wishes by remaining her little boy forever. He was never able to experience the supreme adventure of loving a woman. Is a successful life anything more than the capacity to love? This question lies at the centre of Freud's work; it is also at the heart of Barrie's interrogations and his writing. The Viennese doctor did not explore his own manner of loving; this is perhaps why he could invest so deeply in the exploration and analysis of this fundamental process in human beings. James Matthew Barrie consistently asked himself this question; he knew that he was 'gay, innocent and heartless', and all his books are a testimony to his inability to love.

James Barrie groomed his image with care, but above all he wanted to be loved. He learned this very early with his mother, and sought admiration unceasingly. Persons for whom the reflection of oneself, their image, is of most importance, are afraid to seek the truth because the truth is always a little unflattering. Narcissus remains fascinated by the reflection in the water of a young and handsome boy, until age tarnishes his beauty and he dies unwittingly.

Deep in his heart James Matthew Barrie had a limitless desire for truth. His steadfast courage touches us more than anything else. The writer knows that his job is to provide a good image of his hero, but Barrie is incapable of this, simply because he has decided to 'lend attention to the things that a real biographer normally relegates to the background'.

# CHAPTER 5

# The lost child-adult: a wife as mother

To leave one's mother, one's first love, is no easy matter. Nevertheless, it is a necessary route for a man if he is to encounter that other love, the love of a woman. The lost child, however, is incapable of leaving the mother that he never had and continues to seek her in all women.

James Matthew Barrie left Kirriemuir behind him and he left his mother, but he was never able to cross the border correctly. In London he embarked upon a career as journalist by relating the customs and mores of Kirriemuir, all that he had learned from Margaret. He had tried to make her laugh continuously and, above all, to fulfil this ambitious little woman's dreams of a 'hero son'.

He in fact surpassed all her expectations, as he succeeded in becoming one of London's most famous playwrights, to the point of being knighted by Queen Victoria; he became Sir James Matthew Barrie.

Unlike many other men, James Matthew Barrie knew that he was different, that he was a 'betwixt-and-between' but, despite the lucidity of his writings, he was doubtless unaware of the consequences that his 'state' could have not only on himself, but also on many other people:

He knew he could never be a real human again, but oh! how he longed to play as other children play, and of course there is no such lovely place to play in as the Gardens … The birds brought him news of how boys and girls play, and wistful tears appeared in Peter's eyes.

One of the first things to do to be 'like others' was to get married. Therefore on Monday, 9 July 1894, James Matthew Barrie took Mary Ansell for his wife. The marriage, simple and discreet, was held in the home of the parents, according to Scottish custom. The couple then left for Switzerland on their honeymoon. Two days later, Barrie noted in his diary:

> Our love has brought me nothing but misery.
>
> Boy all nerves. 'You are very ignorant.'
>
> How? Must we instruct you in the mysteries of lovemaking?

## To do like others

Mary Ansell was an actress. Beautiful and seductive, she had been introduced to Barrie as the possible leading role in his second play, *Walker London*. He soon succumbed to her charms, and insisted that she be given the part. Mary appreciated the black humour of the writer, who seldom smiled and ridiculed all he cherished most. She also bore his capricious moods; he could be gregarious and amusing company, but immediately afterwards not open his mouth for days.

Shortly after their meeting, Barrie started a novel called *The Sentimentalist* in which his field of research was based on his relationship with Mary Ansell:

> This sentimentalist wants the girl to fall in love with him, he tyrannizes and dominates her (it works), but he doesn't want to marry her.
>
> She orders clothes for him.—Motherly feelings.
>
> His tenderness (weakness) because he feels for her & keeps the relationship going on because he doesn't want to make her miserable.

When someone marries just to act 'as if', and pretends to feel love whereas, in fact, one is of 'two minds', then catastrophe can be expected.

As Freud said, nature returns, right away with its share of 'hatred'; this is the 'devil' side of Pan.

When I was twenty-one years old, it was 'normal' to become engaged, and all my university friends were already thinking of marriage. I had neither white dresses nor babies in my head; I had to accomplish the destiny that my father had set for me—to become a doctor—I wanted to change the world!

This neither prevented me from being interested in men, nor men from being interested in me! Thus, a young and brilliant engineer, the first man in my life, proposed to me. I was of two minds, but he was so insistent (I also think that a part of me wanted to do like the others) that I said yes. We organised a small family ceremony, but from that day on I began to have terrible nightmares. Every night I witnessed murders, blood, giant spiders hovering above my head until I woke up in a sweat.

This continued until the day I decided to break off our engagement. My former fiancé bought a gun and left for New York to 'end his days'. Fortunately, this dramatisation sufficed, and he was able to continue his life. We remained good friends, and I recovered my dreams of grandeur. It is strange to see how death can come so close when one cheats on feelings.

## The shadow of tragedy

Was it by chance that Barrie's marriage to Mary Ansell took place after a tragic event concerning his younger sister, Maggie? Maggie was engaged to a family friend, the Reverend James Winter. In a gesture of generosity, James Barrie gave the fiancé a horse as a wedding present, but a few days before the ceremony James Winter was thrown by the horse and killed instantly. Maggie reacted as her mother had done in the face of tragedy; she took to her bed and refused to be consoled. Barrie felt terribly guilty, as he had with his mother many years before. He never left her bedside, and shared the tragedy with her. But at the same time, he took notes for a future book—was this a way to protect himself? As if wishing to make amends, he promised his sister he would take care of her for the rest of her life. Fortunately for both, Maggie eventually married her dead fiancé's brother.

James Matthew wanted to be considered 'normal', and marriage offered him the impression of conformity. He was content to escape from his solitude and very proud that men turned their heads to gaze at his pretty wife. He finally felt 'ordinary', yet he could never be a 'husband'.

As time passed, Mary increasingly played the role of mother for him, because he wanted to be spoiled and protected. Although she loved the 'little boy' in him, she naturally expected something else: a man, a lover, a husband, and a father for the child she desired. Alas, while she could share many adventures with him, she was deprived of this one. She wrote later:

> JM's tragedy was that he knew that as a man he was a failure and that love in its fullest sense could never be felt by him or experienced. It was this knowledge that led him to engage in his sentimental philandering. One could almost hear him, like Peter Pan, crowing triumphantly, but his heart was sick all the time.

Little by little, Mary Barrie gave up the hope that James would grow up one day to take his place as a man by her side. She turned her attention to her dogs, until she met a man capable of responding to her female desire. She wrote:

> When love dies, nothing is deader, because even those who have known it one day will deny it, or forget that it existed. Yet in this case, love was never truly forgotten. It was wasted, mistreated. It was stifled and neglected, and then legally thrown into a tomb.

James Matthew Barrie took the news of his wife's liaison with another man as a terrible catastrophe. He would never have believed that such an event was possible, and he begged Mary to deny the rumour. When she retorted that it was true and that she wanted a divorce, he was totally devastated. Without Peter Pan realising it, Wendy had tired of his incorrigible indifference.

A sad child is unaware of the damage he can do to someone he loves. He cannot feel the tragedy because for him everything is an adventure. For instance, Peter was able to fly thanks to the fairy Tinker Bell who guided him everywhere. He considered her as part of his environment, therefore he could hurt her and be unfaithful to her, without ever doubting her feelings for him! Similarly, during the flight to Neverland, he sometimes forgot Wendy's existence completely and went off on an adventure, then failed to recognise her on his return.

Some women tell me that their husbands no longer see them, as if they had melted into the landscape. Others complain that their companion developed a habit of doing whatever he wants, but cannot bear the thought that she take a holiday alone with a female friend.

Many 'Wendies' enjoy playing 'little mother' for their boy husbands. They are able to be glad for him provided that he is happy, even if it is with other women! Mary played Wendy for many years. Jamie was certainly interested in beautiful women, especially when they were accompanied by children, even though he did not fulfil his role as a husband, remaining impassive to the amorous needs of his wife.

## A model family

The fatal meeting with the Llewelyn Davies family seems accidental, but, on closer consideration, it was inevitable! James Matthew and Mary were accustomed to walking with Porthos, their Labrador, in Kensington Gardens. The little man, wearing a huge black cloak, with his pretty wife by his side and the big joyful dog, could not fail to attract the attention of passers-by. On one of these occasions two little boys wearing red berets started a conversation with them.

It so happened that shortly afterwards, Barrie was invited to a soirée at the home of a fashionable lawyer, Sir George Harris, where he noticed a very beautiful woman, Sylvia Llewelyn Davies. As he had accepted the invitation, he was in a sociable mood for once, and very satisfied to find himself seated at a table beside this beautiful woman.

Apart from the photographs and paintings which depict her, Sylvia has been described thus by a contemporary:

> Without being strictly pretty, she has got one of the most delightful, brilliantly sparkling faces I have ever seen. Her nose turns round the corner—also turns right up. Her mouth is quite crooked ... Her eyes are very pretty—hazel and very mischievous. She has

pretty black fluffy hair: but her expression is what gives her that wonderful charm, and her low voice.

During dinner, Barrie was intrigued to see Sylvia putting sweets into her bag, and asked her for whom they were intended. 'It's for Peter,' she replied, as if this were the most natural thing in the world. Thus began a conversation revealing that Sylvia was talking to the man with the persistent cough who amused her children in Kensington Gardens. She was the mother of the boys with the red berets.

'There never was a simpler happier family [than the Darlings] until the coming of Peter Pan,' wrote James Barrie in *Peter and Wendy*. Was he describing his arrival in the Llewelyn Davies family?

Arthur Llewelyn Davies, Sylvia's husband, a young lawyer, brilliant and ambitious, was the offspring of a 'good Protestant family'. Sylvia's parents were George and Emma Du Maurier, a rather bohemian and artistic couple (George Du Maurier was a caricaturist for *Punch*), who saw the funny side of life. Sylvia's mother found Arthur a bit too serious for her daughter, who was so vivacious and extroverted. Nonetheless, he was very handsome.

The Llewelyn Davies family offered James Barrie an ideal opportunity to pursue all his fantasies. After the failure of his life as the husband of a 'normal couple', he could both continue to play with children and seduce a mother.

Ah! If only we could remain gay, innocent, and heartless forever! Did James Matthew Barrie turn to the Llewelyn Davies family, his Darling family, in the hope of achieving this fantasy?

When he met them, Arthur and Sylvia already had three boys: George, aged five; Jack, aged four; and Peter, still a baby. Yet George, the eldest, was not his first 'victim'. Barrie had met other children at his friends' homes, such as Margaret, the daughter of the writer W. E. Henley. She called Barrie 'my friendy', but she pronounced it 'my wendy', which gave rise to the unprecedented Christian name of 'Wendy'.

There were also his two nephews, Charlie and Willie. Charlie was very handsome and intelligent, which greatly pleased the writer. He was equally interested in his anarchistic and deliberately destructive temperament. For Barrie, the character of children was 'inspired as much by the devil as by God'. He revelled in their contradictions, their unlimited appetites, their lack of morality, their self-sufficiency, their ingratitude and their cruelty, alongside the gaiety, the warmth, the tenderness and the sudden waves of emotion, instantly forgotten. Furthermore, he knew very well how to win their affection by behaving in the same way himself.

## Irresistible intrusion

Yet Arthur Llewelyn Davies was reluctant to accept James Matthew Barrie's passion for his sons. He would have liked to have had moments alone with his family when he came home from work in the evening, and he was not always happy to see the little man in his home. To tell the truth, he didn't know how to get rid of him! He also had to resist Barrie's persistent generosity, because the writer was ready to give the children and their parents everything that they could possibly desire!

Barrie did not disguise his great admiration for Sylvia, whom he described in his diary as a 'glorious woman … whom one can trust. No question of sex', he added in parentheses.

No sex! What a comfort for Jamie to know that this woman did not expect that of him. She was close, beautiful, a mother of five boys, and she had a husband whom she loved and who adored her. Jamie enjoyed every moment spent in her company; he took many photographs of her and her sons, and the boys gradually became the heroes of his writing. He wrote about their gestures in his notebooks, each smile, each tear, to bring them later into their true light, the creation of his painful fantasy. Concerning George, for example, the model for the 'little white bird', he wrote: 'I could forgive him everything, except his youth.'

Why did the Darling/Davies family open the window and let this strange little man into their home? Was Sylvia, like Wendy, seduced by the great need for motherly love that she must have unconsciously felt toward James Barrie? Did she give in to the socialite pleasure of playing with the famous playwright and enjoying the flattery of his compliments? She certainly knew nothing of the power of the diabolical conflicts taking place in his tormented mind. Mrs Darling had felt the danger that Peter Pan represented; Sylvia was unaware of it.

At first Jamie remained on the window-sill from where he could observe at leisure, taste, take, and dominate the family. Even if he remained excluded from the lost love of his childhood, this situation enabled him to continue to play, as he had always done, at being everything for his mother, for a mother. On the occasion of Sylvia's fifth wedding anniversary, he wrote her a letter wherein he pretended that it was the very day of his own wedding. He succeeded in going back in time as he had already done in his book *Margaret Ogilvy*—he could not be excluded from such an event!

> Dear Miss Du Maurier,
>
> And so you are to be married tomorrow! And I shall not be present. You know why.
>
> Please allow me to wish you great happiness in your married life. And at the same times I hope you will kindly accept the little wedding gift I am sending you ... It reaches you somewhat late, that is owing to circumstances too painful to go into. It is not a wedding ring, but if you wear it, it could become one.

## The prince of the fairies

Barrie shared his literary successes with 'his family', and especially with Sylvia, whom he once took to Paris for the opening night of the play *Peter Pan*. It was a solitary Arthur, probably a bit unhappy, who wrote to his father:

> I don't know what your arrangements are for Christmas, nor if you are likely to have the Vicarage very full. I should like to come, if possible, bringing one boy or perhaps two ... Sylvia is at present on a trip to Paris with her friends the Barries, by way of celebration of the huge success of Barrie's new play and new book ... they seem to be living in great splendour and enjoying themselves very much.

Was this also Arthur's great regret? 'If only we had not accepted this dinner invitation!' lamented Mr Darling when he discovered that his children had left for Neverland with Peter Pan.

In May 1906, nine years and some months after the famous dinner where they met Barrie, Arthur Llewelyn Davies fell gravely ill; a rare tumour was discovered in his mouth, and an operation deprived him of speech. This tragedy served James Matthew Barrie well, because it enabled him to take root even more solidly in the Davies family.

He visited Arthur, read him the newspapers, and offered him all the services that he needed. Sylvia wrote to her son Michael for his sixth birthday: 'Mr. Barrie is our fairy prince, much the best fairy prince that was ever born, because he is real.'

Jamie was again beside a woman faced with the death of a loved one. Was this a repetition of the tragic moments of his childhood? By becoming so deeply involved in the life of the Llewelyn Davies family, was he trying to impede destiny?

It is always a strange situation when tragedies are repeated, and we find ourselves in the mysterious déjà vu that makes us lose our bearings. I experienced this when I returned to Hungary for the first time with my mother to find the barbed wire fences and soldiers, with machine guns on their hips. We had Canadian passports. After waiting for hours to be 'inspected' I was suddenly seized by two equally violent and contradictory desires: to turn around, go back, and never return; or to jump over the barbed wire screaming, hands stretched to the sky: 'Come on, kill me, let's put an end to this barbarity!' I think that this fantasy satisfied me, because I continued to wait until our turn came.

It is difficult to know what James Matthew Barrie felt during this tragedy: was he divided between the desire to love, to cry, to have pity … and the desire to kill, to possess, to take the place of the father—finally to have his own boys? In Neverland, the only rule is 'kill or be killed', 'eat or be eaten'.

Subsequently the Davies' sons tried to understand the circumstances that had surrounded the death of their father. Peter Davies, as an adult, wrote about gathering family information from various sources of correspondence. His proposed book was curiously called *Morgue*, but he never published it. He commented thus on his parents' relationship with the writer. When the situation became very serious:

> JMB stepped in to play the leading part; and played it in the grand manner … I can sympathize in a way with the point of view that it was the last straw for Arthur that he should have had to accept charity from the strange little genius who had become such an increasing irritation to him in recent years. But on the whole

I disagree. We don't really know how deep the irritation went; and even if it went deep, I am convinced that the kindness and devotion of which JMB gave such overwhelming proof from now on, far more than outweighed all that, and that the money and promise of future financial responsibility he was so ready with—and with what charm and tact he must have overcome any resistance!—were an incalculable comfort to the doomed Arthur as well as to Sylvia in her anguish.

## The outstretched hand

But Jack, the younger brother, felt differently:

> I couldn't but agree with the idea that father had a most cordial dislike of the Bart. I felt again and again that his letters simply blazoned the fact that he was doing all he could, poor man, to put up a smokescreen and leave mother a little less sad and try to show her he didn't grudge the Bart being hale and hearty and rich enough to take over the business … I've no doubt at all he was appreciative, but he was a proud man, and the whole thing must have had a bitter taste for him. He would have been too sweet, and angelical had he liked the little man as well.

Arthur Davies could no longer speak, and he communicated in writing with James Barrie, who hardly ever left his bedside:

> What have the boys been doing? I leave it all in your hands in accordance with Sylvia's wishes. No one has done so much for me as you have. Give me your hand …

Meanwhile, the writer, at the sick man's bedside, continued to take notes, identifying with Arthur:

> A dying man shares fears with a friend that he may break down & blubber at the end—weakness may master him … His idea wd have liked to have children … to live on in them. Speaks to a friend (a father) about the great difference in dying if you have children (yourself living on); if you haven't you go out completely.

Once again, he is installed in the place of the other, the other who is now dying. At the same time, he takes away his children, because it is he who 'would have loved to have children—continues to live in them'. Captain Hook extends his claws, ready to seize the other's treasure.

Peter Davies relates in his private notes the time when the children learned about the death of their father:

> Those words must have penetrated pretty clearly into our immature brains, even though we were not able to understand their full significance. It was, as I remember it, a dull and windy day, and I recollect wandering up to the night nursery and staring out of the window for long minutes in vague wretchedness and gloom, at the grey sea and the distant Gull lightship ... 'A boy's will is the Wind's will' and as likely as not I was digging holes in the sand as usual the next morning. But from that moment on I realized that a disastrous thing had overcome us.

## Act as if …

Despite the shadow of the ineradicable tragedy, life continued after the father's death. Things even seemed to go along 'as if nothing had happened'. The children played and attended school; James Matthew Barrie was always present and contributed considerable financial help. Sylvia tried not to show how much she was suffering. She wrote the following to a close friend one month following her husband's death:

> The little boys are loving and attentive, and I always sleep with George now. It comforts, more than I can say, to touch him, and I feel Arthur must know. He will live again in them and I must find comfort in that until I join him at last.

Two days after the Barries divorced, Peter Davies saw his mother faint and fall in the stairway of the house in Campden Hill Square. The diagnosis was irrevocable: cancer, too near the heart to operate. Yet the pretence must continue; Sylvia must not know the gravity of her state. Her illness was less impressive than her husband's because she did not undergo an operation, but her health declined very rapidly.

Soon she had to be carried in a chair. At Christmas, when the children came home for their holidays, they found their mother confined to her bedroom. Despite the 'as if nothing had happened', they knew that tragedy was striking again.

James Barrie was constantly at Sylvia's side, resuming the role that he had played beside Arthur, three years before. At the same time, he revised his manuscript of Peter and Wendy and took copious notes:

> The dying. Friends around talking about other things. Questions about dying, preparing to die—for the journey.
>
> A play: a man tutors four girls (better than boys?)
>
> A second chance: Beware or you may get what you desire …

Realising what desire? To be at the bedside of a dead mother for the second time, and to feel once again the sadness of a little boy who has lost his mother? Oh! So many lost children, so many lost childhoods; or was it the wish to be finally alone with the boys, playing at being father and mother all at once?

## A dead mother

Sylvia Llewelyn Davies died on 27 August 1910. Her mother, Emma Du Maurier, the doctor, the nurse, and Barrie were at her side on her deathbed. The boys had gone fishing by the river.

Peter Davies remembers (in his memoirs) his return to the house in the late afternoon, and the shock that he felt on discovering the curtains drawn at all the windows. James Barrie awaited him in the entrance, completely broken-hearted, and gave him the news with desperate, incomprehensible words:

> Poor Jimmy! I think it was just as much I that propelled him, as he pushed me, into the room on the left of the entrance hall, where we sat down and cried together. I remember, and wished I didn't, sobbing out 'Mother! Mother!' during that painful scene, and realizing, at the same time that this wasn't altogether in my nature—that, though half involuntary, it was also a half deliberate playing-up to the situation. Playing-up to James Barrie?

Nico, aged seven at the time, approached Sylvia's bedroom with the intention of entering, as usual, at tea-time, but 'he was rudely expelled by one of his brothers, Michael, and fled crying hysterically: "Cruel God! Cruel God."' At the time, George had not yet returned from fishing. As for Jack, he also became angry, but with James Barrie:

> I was taken into a room where [Barrie] was alone, and he told me she was dead. He also told me, which angered me even then, that Mother had promised to marry him and wore his ring. Even then, I thought if it was true, it must be because she knew she was dying. I was then taken in to see her and left with her for a bit. She looked quite natural, as she'd always been so pale, very lovely and asleep.

Had Barrie told the truth, or was it a product of his hyperactive imagination? Did Sylvia seriously consider marriage with the small, strange, faithful creature? We shall never know. But Peter, in his memoirs, felt that a union between Sylvia, still so beautiful at forty-four, widow of the splendid Arthur, and the little man who adored her and who surely dreamt of stepping into Arthur's shoes, would have been 'a true affront to common sense, for any reasonable person'.

Peter had no memory of the funeral but, on the other hand, he remembered that the writer had given them new fishing rods on the same morning:

> And I dare say it worked well enough, and that the new rods helped, as no doubt JMB with generous cunning knew that they would, to do the trick. At any rate, we enjoyed ourselves flogging the little upland streams and hauling out the trout, and putting the horrible worm behind us forever.

'Mrs. Darling was dead and forgotten', wrote James Matthew Barrie at the time in *Peter and Wendy*, while simultaneously watching the boys fish in the rivers!

# CHAPTER 6

# Captain of the lost boys

Peter Pan or Captain Hook? Barrie was finally alone with the lost boys; the sole master of their destiny. Depressed and unsure of himself, he was caught between a whimsical, cocky, and oblivious Peter Pan and a cruel Captain Hook. We have serious reason to be anxious about the future of the Davies boys.

Immediately after Sylvia's death, James Barrie informed the Du Maurier family of his intention of becoming the children's 'tutor'. To ensure that this would happen he had falsified Sylvia's last will by replacing the name 'Jenny', the sister of the governess Mary Hodgson (whom Sylvia wanted to live in her house) with 'Jimmy'! He thereby gave himself the right to consider 23 Campden Hill Square as 'his' home.

Mary Hodgson protested fervently: like Nana with Peter Pan, she believed that the writer was dangerous for the boys. Nor had Emma Du Maurier, the boy's grandmother, ever liked him, and all his generosity and gentleness had not changed her opinion. But, despite this opposition, the family remained powerless in the face of Barrie's unwavering determination.

Once assured of his role as a tutor, he set to it as best he could. Nothing was too fine for 'his boys': the finest holidays, the best leisure activities, the best clothes, and, above all, the best schools, Eton and Oxford, where the élite of English society were trained. James Barrie had never been ashamed of his modest origins (from which he drew inspiration in his writings), but he secretly admired the aristocracy with which he flirted thanks to his literary success. The fact that he was sending 'his boys' to the leading public schools of England gave him tremendous satisfaction.

Yet, despite this tender solicitude James Matthew Barrie irresistibly drew the boys to Neverland, not to enable them to grow up, but to take from them what he himself had lost. In *The Little White Bird*, George, the eldest of the Davies boys, supplied the model of David, the hero. The book is written in the first person by Captain W., 'an old bachelor, pleasant, whimsical and solitary', who is also a writer and who takes regular walks in Kensington Gardens with his dog Porthos. His secret ambition is to have a son whom he could call Timothy. Since he is incapable of realising this wish himself (it would necessitate intercourse with a woman), he wheedles himself into the life of a poor young couple by helping them financially, but in an occult fashion.

When the couple expects a child, the Captain observes the matter closely and, when the father announces that it is a boy, the Captain, to be like him (to be normal) tells him that he also has a son, whose name is Timothy.

## The five brothers

When Sylvia died, George was seventeen years old, and he thought of Barrie as a close friend. Jack was the only one who opposed Barrie's adoption of the boys. Was it because, unlike his brothers, he had never inspired the writer? Nevertheless, he accepted the solution of tutorship by Barrie. Peter was thirteen, and bore the fatal Christian name of Peter Pan. Shortly after their mother's death, he entered Eton, where he was soon subjected to merciless teasing by his classmates, convinced that he was 'the real Peter Pan', until he derived a genuine phobia for the play, calling it a 'terrible masterpiece'.

But it was with Michael that Barrie sustained the most complicated relationship. Michael was born shortly after the playwright's arrival in the Davies family. One could presume that the strange little man seized this opportunity to behave as though Michael were his son. After all, the 'little white bird' furnished a ready-made scenario for him. In any case, this was the opinion of Denis Mackail, a contemporary of Barrie, struck like others by 'Barrie's mesmerizing power, always irresistible when he has made his choice'. According to him, the little boy, lively, intelligent and handsome, represented everything that the magician admired most, and he was undoubtedly his favourite.

Nico, the youngest, aged seven when his mother died, was outwardly the least affected by the disappearance of his parents. He was also charming, extroverted, and affectionate. Like Michael, he considered Barrie neither as a father nor as a brother, but simply as 'just the person I always hoped most would be coming in to see me'.

In the meantime, the writer was preparing *Peter and Wendy*:

> Then [the lost boys] went on their knees, and holding out their arms cried, 'O Wendy lady, be our mother.'
>
> 'Ought I?' replied Wendy blushing. 'Of course, it's frightfully fascinating, but you see … I have no real experience.'
>
> 'That doesn't matter,' said Peter, 'What we need is just a nice motherly person.'
>
> 'Oh dear!' exclaimed Wendy, 'you see I feel that is exactly what I am. Very well, I will do my best.'

## Love and hate

While playing at 'mothers and fathers', which must have satisfied the demonic side of the god Pan, in other words by being what Freud calls the 'archaic father of a primitive horde', Barrie pursued his self-observation, his search for truth. His dreams continued to torment him, and he scrupulously noted them down in his diary; for example, he woke suddenly, petrified with fear, sure of having felt the sheets move:

> I displace my body cautiously and it stops moving. Long pause; then it resumes, pushes me gently—I resist. Pause. The electric lamp is near me; I grind my teeth for courage to turn on the light— queer idea I won't be able to do it—I put out my hand and it is stopped by something limp. No sound of breathing. Then I feel

a stronger pressure to push me out of bed. At last, I flee from the darkness to mother's room [she has been dead many years] and tell her about my degenerate self—thing I have evolved into trying to push me out of bed to take my place. Till that moment of telling, I had no idea what the thing was.

Was this 'degenerate self' of James Matthew Barrie the lost child who continued to weep in the ageing body? It is interesting to note that Freud tells a similar story when he states that where there is love there is hate, that the life wish is accompanied by the wish of death. Where there is construction, there is destruction.

When aggression is blocked by external obstacles or for interior reasons, this state can be experienced as a grave injury, and the force of repression can turn against the subject himself to destroy him … A bit like the crocodile ceaselessly pursuing Hook to devour him …

## Illness à la carte

A little old sad child came to tell me her story. She was so small, with such a gentle voice, that I suspected that she must be very destructive. She told me how her parents had abandoned her at age four after she was hospitalised with a grave illness. She was given up for lost, and her parents, who lived abroad, did not come to see her. But she did not die. Her convalescence lasted many years: she had practically forgotten her family, and spent her time making up stories. One of her favourite games was the story of a girl who was beaten by her mother.

Once cured, she returned to her family, pursued brilliant studies and, later on, married the man of her choice, against her parents' wishes. The marriage was rather a success for her, because she found in her husband a considerable degree of violence which she herself also had, but had never been able to express. She had many children but, by ill luck, each of them nearly died as a baby, either by poisoning or from starvation. Every time, she saved them at the very last minute, when she managed to summon up what remained of her desire to see them survive.

When they became adults, they continued nevertheless to 'please' their mother by being gravely ill from time to time and smoking and drinking. Fortunately, they inherited their father's robust constitution and his violent opposition to their mother, thus enabling them to survive!

Freud was highly interested in the fact that some people continually repeat actions harmful to themselves and to others as if they were pursued by an inexorable fate. He called this a 'demoniacal compulsion to repeat' because, in closely examining the situation, it seemed obvious that this 'fate' had left nothing to chance.

A mother came to see me shortly after the death of her son at the age of twenty-three. She was unable to mourn for him and spoke to me about a black fate that preyed on her family. At the age of ten she lived in England. Vaccinations were not compulsory for the children, and her mother decided not to have them vaccinated. During an epidemic of diphtheria, this woman and her four brothers and sisters fell ill. Her favourite brother, five years younger than herself, died.

Later on, she married and had five children, like her mother, of whom the eldest boy closely resembled the dead brother. Naturally, she named him after her dead brother. When conflict exploded with her husband, she shared her frustrations with her children, ensuring that they took 'her side' against their father. It reminded her of her bad relationship with her own father, who spent his time gardening to avoid family quarrels. Little by little, the eldest son took the place of the 'man' defending his mother. He died choking like the brother, not by diphtheria, but by a tumour of the throat!

Is it possible to mourn a dead child? Is it possible to mourn a dead mother? These losses dig deep into Neverland. Sylvia 'Darling' was dead and forgotten, but everyone acted as if nothing had happened, as if life could simply continue.


## The double

Towards the end of April 1913, Michael also entered Eton. Whereas George had adjusted to his new environment within a few days, Michael was very unhappy, and was terribly homesick. He missed Mary Hodgson. He missed Uncle Jim. But, more than anything, he missed his mother. For three years, Barrie had done his best to replace their mother. He accompanied them to school, played with them at billiards or cricket, and at night he comforted them when they awoke from their nightmares.

But now that Michael was alone, without Barrie to fill his head with other thoughts, he languished for the contact of the 'vanished hands'. He tried desperately to disguise his feelings, hiding behind a shield of reserve, or trying to mask his depression with bleak humour, like that of his tutor. Barrie wrote later: 'I think few have suffered from the loss of a mother as he has done.' In the hope of filling this solitude, he proposed to write every day, instead of once a week, as he did with George. By the time Michael left Eton, 2,000 letters had been exchanged.

The lost child cannot abandon the dead parent. Even if he forgets, if he tries to act as if nothing has happened, he constructs a living tomb within himself; little by little, the tomb and he became one. The lost child behaves like a cannibal: he eats the dead person, and then he feels guilty for having killed him. He must therefore punish himself for his crime; he is tormented, he suffers, but, at the same time, he is avenging himself on the dead person, making the dead person suffer and thus, in a perfectly contradictory way, he derives satisfaction from this suffering.

This is another facet of Hook's vengeance. James Matthew Barrie found his double in this game with himself, and the double was Michael. We have seen how the relationship was based on the confusion between Barrie's imaginary child and the real child. To express these secret feelings, the writer dedicated a book to Michael: *Neil and Tintinnabulum*, the story of a gay, innocent, and heartless little boy, Neil, who, having reached adolescence, loses confidence in himself and becomes a different person, Tintinnabulum.

Michael also fuelled James Matthew Barrie's fantasies in his quest for a double: like Barrie, he was prey to terrible nightmares. This mirror reflecting his own nocturnal life gave Barrie the inspiration for Peter Pan:

> Sometimes, he [Peter Pan] had dreams, and they were more painful than the dreams of the other boys. For hours, he could not get rid of them, and he wept pitifully. They concerned, I believe, the secret of his existence.

## Forbidden to grow up

James Matthew Barrie wanted to play his role as the 'mother' of the boys forever, yet inevitably they grew up. George was already twenty and was infatuated with a young girl, Josephine Mitchell-Innes, daughter of a good family, whom he wanted to marry. Barrie didn't know what to do: in Neverland, it is forbidden to grow up …

This ideology also had real consequences for the play *Peter Pan*, which continued to be performed successfully in London ever since its creation. Pauline Chase, the actress who played the role of Peter Pan, reported to the journal *Peter Pan's Post*:

> Every December a terrifying ceremony takes place before Peter Pan is produced, and this is the measuring of the children who play in it. They are measured to see whether they have grown too tall, and they can all squeeze down into about two inches less than they really are, but this does not deceive the management …

This reminds us of Peter Pan's words about the lost boys: 'When they grow, I kill them.'

On 4 August 1914, Great Britain declared war on Germany. George, Michael, and Nico were on holiday with Barrie in Scotland, far from the news with which all of Europe was burning. George, already enlisted, persuaded his brother Peter to join up with him. While awaiting their call-up, they continued to live as before. The boys fished and took long walks.

On the first day of training, while they were getting ready, George said to his brother: 'Well, young Peter, for the first time in our lives, we're up against something really serious, **** me if we aren't.' Was it the sad child in him who sensed the coming tragedy? Had he picked this destiny for interior reasons? Or was it pure chance?

James Matthew Barrie opened his wings wide to try to protect his lost boys. He was all the more present, generous, and anxious since the danger, on this occasion, came from the outside.

The letters exchanged between George and Barrie at the time let us measure the depth of the relationship between the two men: 'My dear George,' wrote Barrie, 'your letter comes, and I know you are off. It is still a shock to me. I shall have many anxious days and nights too, but I only fall into line with so many mothers.'

The last letter that George received while he was alive was dated 11 March. Barrie advised him of the death, at the front, of Guy Du Maurier, Sylvia's brother: 'Of course I don't need this to bring home to me the danger you are always in …'

George was killed on 15 March 1915 in a column marching to Saint-Eloi. He must have had a premonition of death, because he had just told a comrade next to him that he wanted to be buried where he fell. That evening, he was seated with the others in the trenches when a bullet went through his head, killing him instantly.

A few days after his death, his answer to his tutor's letter arrived; the tone was reassuring, flippant: 'And if I am going to stop a bullet, why should it be with a vital place?' So Peter Pan, standing in grave danger on his rock, exclaiming with a beating heart: 'To die will be an awfully big adventure.'

## Dark, dour, and impenetrable

Was James Matthew Barrie able to mourn George? Or did death help him to recover in his heart the little boy that he had known in Kensington Gardens?

After the death of the eldest, he clung even more to Michael; 'the dark, dour and impenetrable' as he called him, but Michael changed and escaped from him too, and Barrie dreaded the time when the young man would no longer need him.

The lost child cannot live without his double. Just as he had to renounce having a mother for himself, he always needs a presence to feel that he exists. If the double leaves him, he dies. We can understand why Peter Pan needed the lost boys and why he hated to see them grow up!

After two difficult years at Eton, Michael was hardened, or at least he had composed a nonchalant facade to mask his real feelings, but everyone knew about his depressed state. One of his closest friends, Robert Booth, was convinced of the evil influence that Barrie exerted on the young man:

> Michael took me back to Barrie's flat a number of times, but I always felt uncomfortable there. There was a morbid atmosphere about

it. I remember going there one day, and it almost overwhelmed me, and I was glad to get away. We were going back to Oxford in Michael's car, and I said, 'It's a relief to get away from that flat,' and he said, 'Yes it is.' But the next day he'd be writing to Barrie as usual …

The two men established a relationship considered unhealthy by Michael's entourage: not homosexual, but morbid and beyond the limits of ordinary affectivity. When Barrie was in a dark mood, he tended to drag the young man down with him, as Booth related:

I remember once coming back to the flat with Michael and going into the study, which was empty. We stood around talking for about five minutes, and then I heard someone cough: I turned around and saw Barrie sitting in the inglenook, almost out of sight. He'd been there all the time, just watching us … he was an unhealthy little man, Barrie; and when all is said and done, I think Michael and his brothers would have been better off living in poverty than with that odd, morbid little genius.

Did Michael try to escape the claws of his tutor? After Eton, he no longer wanted to continue his studies and dreamt of living as an artist in Paris, like his grandfather Du Maurier. On the contrary, James Barrie wanted Michael to go up to Oxford. It was Michael who finally gave in to please Barrie, because this was vital for him. As a reward, he was given a car and a little house.

The other Davies children more or less cut themselves off from the writer. At the age of nineteen, Peter had been sent to the heart of the very worst conflict of the war, the Battle of the Somme. He returned two months later, deeply traumatised, and affected by moral wounds from which he never recovered.

With George dead, and his parents vanished, Peter lived for two years outside of time, filled with fear, obsessed by the memory of mud and mutilated bodies, and he never returned to the Neverland of James Matthew Barrie. He set up house with a woman who was twice his age, and this deeply shocked his tutor, and was opposed by everyone, including Mary Hodgson, who for once agreed with Barrie and shared his disappointment.

Jack also escaped by marrying Geraldine Gibb. Barrie, who maintained a rather bad relationship with the 'intruder', nevertheless used her finally to get rid of Mary Hodgson, the boys' beloved governess. She could not bear the presence of the young wife and never spoke to her directly. Barrie exploited the situation by installing Gerrie as the mistress of the house in Campden Hill Square. He then pretended to ignore the rising tension and wrote to Mary with great tenderness when she offered her resignation. He had won: in Neverland, one kills or is killed!

## History repeats itself

In the summer of 1918, James Barrie had an important new encounter: 'a second chance'? As with Sylvia, it happened during a dinner. The young woman (thirty years old, as Sylvia had been at the famous soirée) was Cynthia Asquith. She was married to a solicitor (like Arthur), and was the mother of two boys; Michael, the younger, was the same age as George had been. Cynthia nourished ambitions, especially the desire to make the most of her beauty and her charm. Her husband, unsuccessful professionally, had just abandoned his solicitorship to try his chance in the artistic professions. She needed to earn money. James Barrie offered her a job as a secretary with a high salary and great latitude in her working hours.

Before accepting, she sounded out a number of friends on the writer's personality. She wrote to her friend Sir Walter Raleigh, who answered:

> Why not? But take care you don't kill the golden goose by curbing his sentimentality. Not that it is really sentimentality. More often, for he has a cruel side—it's a Pan that failed.

Desmond MacCarthy, another close friend, congratulated her for taking the post:

> It seems to me … you like being adored—a Dulcinea is a necessity to Barrie. Sentiment is only irritating to an onlooker, and when it is combined with playfulness and real kindness and springs from a cold detached heart, it is a delicate tactful thing, delightful to

receive. Barrie, as I read him, is part mother, part hero-worshipping maiden, part grandfather, and part pixie with no man in him at all. His genius is a coquettish thing, with just a drop of benevolent acid in it sometimes.

The professional relationship between Cynthia and James Barrie was soon transformed into a sincere friendship. But Bob Asquith did not share his wife's admiration for the playwright. He hated his plays and had no sympathy for the man. It is likely that his active resistance (quite different from the resignation of Arthur Davies) and Cynthia's strong personality containing a large dose of egoism prevented history from repeating itself. James Matthew Barrie never held over the Asquiths and their children the power that he had over the Davies.

It is true that 'his boys' still occupied a very large place in his life. Michael was pursuing his studies at Oxford, where he had formed a deep friendship with a young man named Rupert Buxton, depressed like him. Their entourage worried about the influence on Michael of this boy, who was exceptionally intelligent, but sombre, saturnine, and suicidal.

On Thursday, 19 May 1921, James Barrie was putting on his cloak and hat and was ready to leave the house when he found a reporter from a London daily on his doorstep, requesting an interview on the drowning. The drowning? Two Oxford students, Rupert Buxton and Michael Davies, had just disappeared while swimming in the Thames at Sandford pool. Their bodies had not yet been found, but there had been witnesses. The water was very calm at the time of the accident, and the two boys were in each other's arms. Many people thought it was a double suicide.

The story made the headlines of all the English papers, with eloquent titles and commentaries:

The tragedy of Peter Pan: Sir JM Barrie's Loss of An Adopted Son:
There is something of the wistful pathos of some of his own imaginings in the tragedy which has darkened the home of Sir James Barrie. The young men, Mr Michael Llewelyn Davies and Mr Rupert EV Buxton … were drowned near Stanford bathing

pool, Oxford, yesterday. The two undergraduates were inseparable companions. Mr Davies was only twenty and Mr Buxton 22 … The 'original' of Peter Pan was named George, who was killed in action in March 1915 … Now both boys who are most closely associated with the fashioning of Peter Pan are dead …

After this drama, James Barrie shut himself up and refused to see anyone. Michael was buried in Hampstead Cemetery, near the tomb of his parents. A few weeks earlier, Barrie had written in his diary:

Death: One who died is only a little ahead of the procession, all moving that way. When we round the corner, we'll see him again. We have only lost him for a moment because we fell behind, stopping to tie a shoelace.

On 5 April 1960, Peter Llewelyn Davies, publisher, left the Royal Court Hotel, London, crossed Sloane Square, descended the stairs to the Underground and threw himself under a train. The tragedy of Peter Pan once again hit the London headlines. James Matthew Barrie's three favourite boys, each in his own way, had lived 'the biggest of all adventures'.

Was it fate? Or did little Jimmy really believe in a 'second chance'? This question always remained at the centre of James Matthew Barrie's thoughts, and it assumed the most varied forms in his plays. In *The Will*, for example:

Purdie: It isn't accident that shapes our lives.
Joanne: No, it's Fate.
Purdie: It's not Fate, Joanna. Fate is something outside us. What really plays the dickens with us is something in ourselves. Something that makes us go on doing the same sort of fool things, however many chances we get … Something we are born with … Shakespeare knew what he was talking about …
The fault, dear Brutus, is not in our stars,
But in ourselves, that we are underlings.

# CHAPTER 7

# Folded wings

One evening, just after the magic moment of story time, my son, only three then, said to me: 'Mummy, I am so sad because I know that you and Daddy will die one day. I'll never be able to laugh now like I used to.' Although his laughter never ceased, something did change from then on. Sometime later, however, he was just as capable of exclaiming flippantly: 'Mummy, when you will be dead, you'll leave me all your money, won't you?'

It is quite extraordinary to realise how lightly children can speak of death. When playing, Wendy and her brothers had no difficulty imagining that they had just met their dead father in the forest. Freud realised that only children could speak of death so lightly, threatening to kill off anyone, even the people they love. Adults, he says, even if they know that death is the natural culmination of life, repress the idea and try to act as if death could be eliminated. In fact, the unconscious ignores death; it cannot possibly picture its own end.

We pretend to be immortal, as if nothing could ever happen to us. I know today that my father was convinced he was protected, as with many heroes, the gods were on his side. My mother told me about a maxim that always circulated in the family about 'the Kanitz guardian angel'. This may be why our change of name made her so unhappy.

The Kanitz guardian angel was sufficient for my father; he needed nothing else.

## Little criminal

Where lies the danger? When we think that death is possible? Or, on the contrary, when we find ourselves immortal, among the gods? It is perhaps these feelings that appear when we truly dread death … Is it the fear of wanting to kill someone we love?

Unlike the fairy-tale giant who can make things disappear at the drop of a hat, the lost child cannot just kill off anything he wants because he has already experienced death or the loss of love in reality. For him, losing love is equivalent to losing life; he is faced with the danger of disappearing himself. Upon becoming an adult, the lost child is often unable to love himself, since he feels guilty of committing a crime, even if he ignores what it is.

A man came to see me one day. He had recently become a father, and although he was very happy, he was shocked by the presence of a paradoxical and irrepressible need to hurt his baby. This situation made him feel so guilty and desperate that when he asked me for help it was almost a threat: he was convinced that he would end his days in prison. Faced with the urgency of the situation and the turmoil of the man, I had to accept, but I also noted my own ambivalent feelings. I should have recoiled before such a despicable act, and yet I was overcome by a deep sympathy for this man. Besides, I couldn't help seeing the baby in him.

This man could only experience the surface of his being. Inside he felt only emptiness. In his mind there was a complete void of his childhood memories. Above all, he dreaded that a void be disturbed by noises: horns, fireworks, and cars. A violent and unexpected sound could make him lose control, and break out like a madman. His baby's cries also triggered these uncontrollable reactions.

His family told him about a brother, two years younger, who died when he himself was four. He had no memory of this. My feeling was that once again the secret lay in the inability to remember.

The Neverland of this lost child was so distant that he needed his mother's help to reach it. It is uncommon for mothers to come to me when the lost child is an adult. One day, I received a call from his mother. She wanted to tell me something that she had never been able to tell her son and felt that it would help him: 'When the little one died, my husband went mad with grief; he was unrecognisable, he couldn't bear the sight of his older son, the one he still had, and he pronounced these terrible words: "Why isn't it he who died?" Sometime later, I found, my son in an armchair, all alone. He was crying and said: "Mummy, will I never see my brother again?" I answered that he must not cry; his brother was in heaven with the angels and that there are other children in the family, and that we will not talk about it anymore.'

I encouraged the old woman to tell the story to her son, as he was now an adult, he could bear it. It was, after all, returning something that belonged to him. Alas, the mother was unable to turn back upon these painful years and asked me to do it in her stead.

In a later session, when we evoked the image of the tragic little figure seated alone in his armchair, the man burst out sobbing. For the first time, he was able to cry about his story and spoke these words: 'My baby! My poor little child, now I understand everything!' The re-enactment of his childhood drama helped this man to experience feelings again. From then on, he could give up the violent impulses that assaulted him.

## Tears of absence

It took me years to recognise that our story had been a tragedy. I was convinced that we had lived through a great adventure, and that my father had died as a hero. My mother, more conservative, said that it was fate. She had her own way of playing with destiny; she constantly imagined how things would have occurred 'if only'. If 'only' they had left Hungary with my father when she was twenty and he thirty … If she had married Zoltan, and not Pista … If she had remained in Italy at the age of nineteen … If she had been born a boy rather than a girl … If her mother had let her die …

We took long walks on Sundays, during which we spoke of the past and the future. I didn't like the 'ifs'; I found it too sad to have regrets! I preferred 'when': when I grow up … when I finish my studies … when I have money … Then we made plans, I flew off for a thousand adventures and I dragged my mother along with me, where she could find her lost dreams again.

We also cried. At the time, my mother worked hard, and she had to leave me alone in the evenings. My brother was often absent. I spent hours in the semi-darkness in the armchair where my father used to relax, listening to music. I had a cat who loved Mozart. He licked my tears while we consoled each other.

My father died in the spring. It was now winter, probably close to Christmas. It was snowing heavily, and when the sun went down the long blue shadows became menacing. I had just come inside from playing with my friends. My mother was not yet home from work. The apartment was dark and empty as I waited for her with my eyes peeled to the window. A white mass covered everything; only a few street lamps broke the monotony of the desolate space. After an hour or two I broke down and cried desperately, convinced that my mother would never come home, perhaps she was dead as well … I had just given up, could hardly see my eyes were so swollen, when suddenly I saw a tiny black spot emerging in the distant whiteness. The spot grew and made its way with difficulty in the deep snow. The tiny black spot was my mother!

The tears of that evening returned from time to time in my life, and the feeling of total despair that invaded me then remain buried in the depths of Neverland.

As time passed, we wept less. Life bore me towards other adventures. My mother henceforth claimed to live only for us. Her life as a woman was finished; she was nothing else but a mother. What did she expect from me? I had taken the place of my father. As he had instructed me, I took care of her. He had no confidence in my brother.

How to grow up? How to become a woman? These questions did not concern me; I was too busy finding ways to realise my father's dream: 'Dr Katalin Kanitz', the dream that had become my most cherished possession. Much later, when I began delving into Neverland, I found therein the pathetic image of a little girl striking a coffin with all her strength to find what she had lost … My father had carried away what I needed to become a woman.

So, I took what remained: his dreams, his words, and the memory of his warm hands. My dead father sustained me in my flight towards life. Without knowing it, I drew my strength from the secret pact signed between us. He left me with a contract that he could not terminate, because he had become silent and because all the unconscious speech was on my side. I was 'my father's daughter', armed with the desire to conquer the world.

## Peter Pan's baby teeth

When a lost child begins to grow up, he is often very responsible, concerned with the well-being of his parents, of his brothers and sisters. You see him at the head of the team, organising the next game; he picks up the weakest; he has an answer for everything. Above all, if he sees someone despondent, depressed, resourceless, the lost child runs to help him, to try to cheer him up. The lost child becomes a social worker, the lost child becomes a doctor, and the lost child becomes a psychoanalyst. Who can say that the lost child has not grown up? He is independent, he is full of energy, and he is the parent of his parents. Yet if we look closely at his smile, we find that he still has his baby teeth!

At age sixteen, I was earning a living and saving for my university studies. I did theatre, I had many friends, and I was happy to be alive. I had romantic affairs, enough for my taste and to nourish my mother with my reports. I told her everything; she participated fully in my life. The only dark spot in my existence was our relationship with my brother and his wife.

After my father died, my mother, not having enough courage to start a life alone with me, had agreed to share my brother's house. Little by little, the situation became untenable and yet it lasted. My brother was very violent at times, and I learned to fear and hate him.

Did he feel that he had to replace my father? I had two men in my life: a dead hero, enclosed in my heart, and a living devil in real life. This dual situation surely sustained the Neverland deep within me, and did not facilitate my capacity to grow up.

Freud has shown that the little girl, in love with her father, expects him to give her a child; but she finally realises that this is an impossible dream and she has to give up this hope and find another man, who will love her and whose child she will bear. This is essential for the little girl to become a woman.

But when a father dies before his little girl can let go of this hope, she may be so violently disappointed that she has no alternative but to lock this dream forever in Neverland, so that the violent feelings will not destroy everything, including herself. I reserved my anger and hatred for my brother, because he had such talent to attract them; therefore, I could dream of a hero that I would meet one day somewhere else, I knew not where.

I always knew that I would leave Canada one day and return to Europe, even if a return to Hungary were impossible. Hungary was the place of Neverland, nourished by my mother's stories, and filled with all my childhood dreams. It was a distant land, far beyond China, even beyond the planet Mars … I knew that I had to return to the east, to re-cross the Atlantic, discover France … I did not yet know that once again I would turn to the past to find what I had lost …

The beginning of my stay in Paris was a return to perceptions of boundless pleasure: everything attracted me—the smells, the colours, the people, the street corners, and the words. I had come to learn French, the third language that would finally unite two separate parts of me: the English head and the Hungarian heart. Thanks to this 'psychic union' I was slowly able to speak about myself, to think and feel at the same time.

I also reconnected with members of my father's family. Was I recouping a part of Neverland? At the time, my thinking was totalitarian—things were either 'good' or 'bad', 'black' or 'white' … I had not yet put anything in order! So when something was good, everything was good. In France, everything was good!

The fact that I changed countries and had placed an ocean between my mother and myself certainly gave me the impression of growing up. This is often the strategy of the lost child: to leave home and venture far away, to return transformed, adult, without having been forced to experience the painful separation every day. Flying off to Europe enabled me, unwittingly, to retain deep nostalgia for my mother and to continue on my father's route: the route to Neverland.

Toronto … Paris … Geneva … All exiled persons land in Geneva sometime or other. Switzerland: clean and organised, strange and mysterious, unbearable … I knew no one in Geneva, I lived alone, and it was up to me to build my life. Did I have to go that far to escape from parental desire and find myself? I could still flee. But something prevented me from letting go. What if 'the difficulty of living' were the biggest adventure of all? I was obstinate, and I would not give up! But in Switzerland I lived through moments of solitude, of despair, bursts of tears, as before.

## The isle of origins

I do not know how the idea of consulting an 'analyst' materialised. For the first time, I realised that I was sad and that something weighed on my story; adventures were not enough; I wanted the truth, my truth. Only I needed to speak in my mother tongue, because the key to Neverland lies in the hollow of the earliest words.

'What can I do for you?' he asked me. He looked and sounded like someone I had known a long time ago. He was bald, like my father, and he rolled his 'r's … All good.

But I was frightened. I did not want to do an 'analysis', as they say, nor anything very long, or very expensive … just enough to … Strange, this man behind me who says nothing. He does it on purpose. I cannot cross the border of intimacy. I am unable to speak to him in Hungarian. Yet one day, without any apparent reason, and without even realising it, I used my ancestral language. The dreams start flowing as from a secret spring unknown to me. Dreams of a large and dark apartment where I see two birds painted on the ceiling, signs of fate, a house cut in two, the revolution, a bomb, I bleed, my mother runs to help me …

What do I expect from the 'shrink'? His silences let me progress at my own pace. But he is not always silent. He tries to point to the road; he offers me some keys. Can I understand the enigma of my story? Neverland opens up, especially at night. I am at the Hungarian border. No one knows it yet, but there is a war on between the French and the Americans. There are a great number of tents, and I am in the middle. The soldiers are killing each other, but I succeed in escaping, thanks to a bomb that I clasp in my hand! I hide behind a tent. I am in a forest, and I meet my father. He had left long before and, this time, it's true, it's not a dream he is really there, but he is ill, he has to be careful because he will probably die; we have very little time to spend together and we have things of the greatest importance to tell each other. But what were we speaking about? I don't know … I wake with the feeling of his presence strongly embedded in me. And then comes the tiredness, the greyness—nostalgia for the absolute …

The old notebooks of the Swiss period contain writings from very different times: dreams, thoughts, cries of solitude. Finally, two pages that I cannot remember having written:

> She tried, but the words would not come, could not come. He loved her, he had said it, and he had written it: 'Please, only a few lines, if you knew how your silence hurts me.' As a child, as she had often asked herself whether one could simply jump out of one's skin, leave everything and start over. 'If I were not I, who would I be?' No one could answer her.
>
> One day it happened. It frightened her at first, but, little by little, the feeling became pleasant, a powerful feeling of freedom. She had succeeded in leaving her body.
>
> Subsequently, she often excelled in provoking this feeling of absence/presence, even when she was in the company of others. It was as if she saw everything from very far; the bodies, words and gestures lost their essence. Nothing had any meaning, and she seemed to float in a very pleasant vacuum.
>
> But, at about the age of sixteen, she lost this gift. At present, it was no more than a memory.

It is strange that this text should fall into my hands, as I now write … That I finally agree to fold my wings to examine the Neverland of my story. To fix words, to take images designed to persist, is a way to kill … to accept that Neverland will emerge from the shadows, that the past is past, and that what is lost is lost forever …

I understand today that this text, written twenty years ago, was already addressed to my father. The word impossible to say was the word 'farewell', farewell to my father.

I now write it on these pages, and I no longer tear them up, but I offer them to the memory of a lost child.

# Neverland today

*This world is but a canvas to our imagination.*

—Henry David Thoreau

Neverland, painted onto the canvas of our imagination, is an all-powerful place where we are masters of space and time. Is it a symbol of being one with the mother, in synergy with her body and mind? The consequence of the trauma of separation at birth for mother and child may result in an unconscious desire to search for the long lost 'utopia' of symbiotic existence and never want to 'grow up'. A child's 'megalomania' as to his own omnipotence can be understood as only 'demanding the return of a state that once existed, "those good old days" in which they were all-powerful'.[1]

It is not surprising that 'story telling' makes us feel invincible, skilled in fashioning our world into a Neverland. We are often unaware that our stories may take us too far, outside the limits of what is possible. An unconscious narrative at the turn of the century encouraged many to feel that leaving behind the 1900s was closing the door on two world wars and other massacres …

---

[1] S. Ferenczi (1913). Stages in the development of the sense of reality. In: J. Borossa (Ed.), *Selected Writings: Sándor Ferenczi*. Penguin, London, 1999.

The beginning of the twenty-first century opened with a new story, the vision of One Globalised World. No more question of Russia versus the Free World; the big bear toppled and the dream of universal, globalised capitalism filled the hearts of many. Eastern European countries were now eager to join the 'Western World', and Hungary was one of the first to do just that. My childhood Neverland opened and I flew back without hesitation.

My joy was boundless when I opened the door of the new Budapest apartment situated a few steps away from where I was born. I must have felt very powerful to take myself so far back into the Neverland of my childhood. Did I think that I could repair our exile, the loss of our home, my mother's tears, and my father's death? Although I visited Budapest under the communist regime, I had not imagined really living there. It was thanks to a friend, sensitive to my story of exile, that I discovered the perfect apartment near the Danube and St. Steven Park where I had played as a child. I suppose it was my version of Kensington Gardens.

I bought the apartment from an 'exiled child', an American-Hungarian, who fled with his parents at age three. His initial hesitations forced me to persevere all the more to make my dream come true.

The bureaucratic and financial arrangements took almost one year and when the moment came for the lawyer to give me the keys, she could not find them. We had to fetch a locksmith to break the lock on the door! Chance had it that we drove into Vadasz Utca (Hunter's Street) right by the Kanitz Printing Business. Suddenly the car jolted to a stop and just managed to avoid crashing into a bulldozer that blocked the passage. The lawyer began swearing in Hungarian then paused abruptly, realising that she was not alone. 'What in the ... are they doing blocking traffic!'

I had been daydreaming, lost in my thoughts about the new apartment, when I looked up to realise that the street was very familiar. Suddenly a violent scream burst forth from somewhere, and it took me a few seconds to realise that it was from my throat! 'It's our building, our printing firm!' They were demolishing the Kanitz C. and Sons that my great ancestors had built in 1848. I was in such shock that I couldn't stop trembling, but I didn't cry. The lawyer stared at me with surprise, re-started her car, and we rushed away quickly from the murderous scene. A few minutes later the locksmith was breaking into my future apartment!

I shrugged off the symbolic entry into Neverland. Nothing could stop me now, not the pigeon dirt covering the floors, the cockroaches scurrying at night, the lamps to be installed or the empty rooms waiting to be furnished. Once the lock was broken, the space revealed itself and the rooms burst with light. The high ceilings were immediately familiar, filling me with an uncanny joy that was beyond comprehension. Three large empty rooms created an impression of freedom and infinite space. The one piece of furniture that had survived was a worn wooden chair, painted white, displaying the wounds of time. I immediately fell in love with the chair. By adding a bed and a small table, I was able to move in and stay for a month.

A first night anywhere is special and often wakeful. Here I fell asleep right away, only to be aroused suddenly by the sound of heavy boots and shouting. I sat up sweating with fear, listening hard, but there was only silence. After drinking some water, and walking back to bed while avoiding stepping on some scampering insect, strange pictures rippled and billowed like transparent curtains before my eyes. Soldiers in uniforms, crowds of people moving silently, my mother sitting in a bare room crying, a candle flickering against a grey wall. A shadow slowly covered my sunny Neverland. How could I possibly come back to live in this place where my father had been arrested, dragged away to the camps, my aunt and uncle murdered in Mauthausen? I remember nothing. I was only a baby. My brother, who usually never spoke about his childhood, in a recent conversation described what he had seen on this street:

> Mother sent me down to buy some groceries at that store on your street, the one that is still there. As I was nearing the corner I saw police and soldiers rounding up people with their hands on their heads. I was so frightened, I turned around and ran home!

During a later visit, he told me that there had been a large hole where the school now stands:

> It was filled with dead bodies and the smell was unbearable! I used to run past holding my nose.

My brother was the oldest; I was just a happy baby bathing in my parents' love. The light, the smell of the air, the river glistening in the sun, the sounds of my mother tongue, and the taste of paprika were all reminders of my lost paradise. I was bringing back my 'baby self' to Budapest but did not realise it at the time. On the contrary, it all seemed very 'grown up' and business-like to be buying back the apartment we lost when we flew out the window and landed in exile. It is difficult to describe the pleasure I had in furnishing the empty rooms with antiques bought in shops around the corner. Did I imagine these to be the pieces from our apartment?

When Neverland is full of stories meant to repair past losses, the pleasure of rehabilitation is unlimited, and this is what I experienced with 'Budapest' found again. Although my existence continued elsewhere, my fantasy of life in Neverland persevered, spinning wonderful tales of desire and missed childhood now to be experienced.

'When I retire, I will spend six months here and six months there …' I promised myself.

The year 2001 was the beginning of a new century. Curiously enough, parallel to the purchase of the Budapest apartment, 2001 marked the publication of a book that I wrote with a journalist friend called *Cruel Tales of Globalisation*.[2] The end of the 'cold war' opened up the fantasy of 'one world' wherein countries would be united by a common interest—global capitalism. The book was to be a *manifesto* warning against the dangers of 'omnipotence' of *One* World.

Sigmund Freud cautioned us a long time ago that the tragedy of man is the fact of being born immature, dependent on its parents for existence. At birth the baby continues to feel at 'One' with the mother, and this 'all-powerful' state is important for survival. With the process of growing up the child confronts the principle of reality, 'no one is all-powerful'. The psyche continues to navigate between the desire for omniscience and the realisation that it is not possible. The road to maturity is finding a delicate balance between feeling 'all-powerful' and fearing 'impotence', being powerless, incapable of acting.

---

[2] K. Kelley-Lainé and D. Rousset, *Contes Cruels de la Mondialisation*, Bayard Press, Paris, 2001.

My return to Budapest, the 'Neverland' of my 'lost childhood' seemed to coincide with the unification of 'our World' into one globalised entity. Was 'globalisation' also built on the ashes of loss—not only the objective ruins of buildings, bridges, and houses resulting from the two World Wars, but also psychic, spiritual, and philosophic loss, the belief systems of human societies? Jeremy Rifkin in his book *Entropy, A New World View* states: 'The need to establish an order to explain the how and why of daily existence has been the essential cultural ingredient of every society. The most interesting aspect of a society's world view is that its individual adherents are, for the most part, unconscious of how it affects the way they do things and how they perceive the reality around them.'

He enumerates the beliefs of Americans that the world is progressing toward a valuable state as a result of the accumulation of human knowledge and techniques—that the individual exists as an autonomous entity, that nature has an order to it, that scientific observation is objective, that human beings are naturally competitive, etc. According to Rifkin, this omnipotent vision of the human condition is soon to be questioned by the increasing knowledge of the effects of entropy on human activity: 'Entropy is the measure of the extent to which available energy in any subsystem of the universe is transformed into an unavailable form ... therefore the laws of thermo-dynamics provide the overarching scientific frame for the unfolding of all physical activity in this world.'[3] The emerging environmental crisis is the visible result of the law of entropy.

Sally Weintrobe, a fellow of the British Psychoanalytical Society, writes about 'globalizing the neoliberal way' resulting from the neoliberal ascendancy in the 1980s, causing the spread of a monolithic consumerist culture across the globe, loosely known as the 'American way of life'. She goes on to say that to live on Planet Earth in the twenty-first century economists must challenge omnipotent thinking and accept that there are limits to growth.[4]

The Reader may ask: 'What has this to do with Peter Pan and Neverland?'

---

[3] J. Rifkin, *Entropy, A New World View*, Bantam Books, NY, 1981.

[4] S. Weintrobe, *Psychological Roots of the Climate Crisis*, Bloombury, NY, 2021.

Neverland is the fruit of 'omnipotent' desires of stopping time to re-live, and to catch up with 'lost childhood'. Barrie is ambivalent about Neverland:

> During the day we can have hundreds of adventures in the Neverland and emerge as the hero each time. But at nightfall suddenly the island's scenery assumes new contours. Familiar objects appear bizarre, wild animals emerge from their lairs. The queen turns into a huge tentacular spider. Father and mother disappear, and we are suddenly tiny and defenceless. Some people have known the Neverland at night, and prefer to forget it. Others return to it with great pleasure, to re-experience the child they left behind, whose memory becomes indispensable for the continuity of living.

Does psychoanalysis have a place in our globalised world of Neverland? In a recent study of the riveting consequence of global capitalism Teresa Brennan[5] enumerates the devastating effects of the deregulation of space and time on human beings. Fast-moving global capitalism employs numerical systems to enable constant adjustment to new technologies that replace 'slow' human beings. The speed of change has taken its toll on the human psyche and psychoanalysts' consulting rooms are rapidly filling with increasing numbers of patients unable to adapt to this 'Brave New World'.

According to the sociologist Zygmunt Bauman[6] the process of modernisation is one of 'melting the solids' and our globalised world is in a state of liquid flux. Liquidity implies 'lightness' and 'weight-lessness', and is associated with mobility and inconstancy. Our entrance into the twenty-first century of globalised capitalism is now forcing us to recognise the revolutionary effects of liquefaction at all levels of society.

The weightlessness of 'liquid modernity' reminds us of Peter Pan's Neverland, where everything is constantly moving in the same direction. If anyone stops (solidifies?), everyone falls down. Peter Pan,

---

[5] T. Brennan, *Globalization and its Terrors*, Routledge, London, 2003.
[6] Z. Bauman, *Liquid Modernity*, Polity Press, Cambridge, 2000.

however, flies away from time to time to an 'old' world where mothers tell stories to their children. Liquid modernity erases boundaries, limits, and distinctions, not only between public and private, but also between reality and desire. The creation of 'desire' becomes one of the essential functions of consumerism, replacing the twentieth century notion of 'need'. Desire is now giving way to a more flexible dream of self-expression, which is gradually being replaced, by a quasi-'addictive' level of consumerism.

'Young, innocent, and heartless' Peter Pans are conquering today's Neverland. They seduce naïve youth and adult populations with their clever inventions. Like Peter Pan many are originally lost children convinced of unlimited powers capable of persuading the world of the inevitability of their creations. Although their original intentions may have been generous and free of charge for the service of humanity, the necessity to join the global capitalist grid became rapidly obvious. They are now congratulated as the most important and wealthiest people in the universe.

The titles of a number of critical works on this development reflect the nature of the new Neverland:

> *You are the Product; The Attention Merchants from the Daily Newspaper to Social Media, How our Time and Attention is Harvested and Sold; Chaos Monkeys Inside the Silicon Valley Money Machine; Move Fast and Break Things: How Facebook, Google and Amazon Have Cornered Culture and What it Means for All of Us …*

Captain Hooks are also popping up in a number of places. Many claim that democracy is in danger as voters give power to leaders with hooks for hands, cavernous looks, and who treat their men as dogs. Are aggressive, totalitarian leaders elected to protect populations from the dangerous side of Neverland? The crocodile lurks in perilous waters.

In 1998, nine years after the fall of the Berlin Wall that marked the end of communism in Eastern Europe, the Hungarian people nominated a young, powerful Peter Pan to lead their country. He was re-elected in 2010, and after his re-election in 2018 he revealed his plan to lead the country as Prime Minister until 2030. Time has enabled him to strengthen his control and power as an illiberal head of state, transforming him into Captain Hook. Thousands of young people are abandoning ship and fleeing toward new horizons in other lands.

On 27 November 2019, a pandemic risk was detected in the city of Wuhan, China. On 17 March 2020, the French government decreed a national lockdown. My travels to Neverland had become less frequent for some time. This was twenty years later, and my dream of living in Neverland for six months had not materialised. Gradually it was a friend, during his frequent stays, who was enjoying the beauty of my Budapest apartment.

Hindsight tells me that an unconscious letting go of the past was gradually taking place. Little by little Budapest lost the childhood memory magic, so powerful at the beginning of Neverland time. Perhaps the 'liquid nature' of society was taking over and indeed, just as with Paris, Budapest was increasingly 'Americanised'.

All of a sudden, the decision to sell the apartment became evident. Friends were very surprised: 'How can you … almost how dare you … that place is so important!' but I was very determined. After contacting a lawyer, I began selling and giving away furniture, keeping only a few lamps, paintings, and the weatherworn white chair. At last I found the mover who would transport the pieces that I had chosen to keep.

Finally I closed the door … for the second time, forever, without tears.

# Bibliography

Barrie, J. M. (1896). *Margaret Ogilvy*. London: Hodder and Stoughton.

Barrie, J. M. (1906). *Peter Pan in Kensington Gardens*. London: Hodder and Stoughton.

Barrie, J. M. (1980). *Peter Pan*. London: Hodder and Stoughton.

Barrie, J. M. (The Works of J. M. Barrie). *Tommy and Grizel*. London: Cassell.

Barrie, J. M. (The Works of J. M. Barrie). *Sentimental Tommy*. London: Cassell.

Birkin, Andrew (2003). *J. M. Barrie and the Lost Boys*. London: Yale University Press.

Freud, Sigmund (1931). Letter to the Burgomaster of Pribor. In: *Standard Edition Vol. 21*, p. 259. London: Hogarth.

Freud, Sigmund (1936). *New Introductory Lectures on Psycho-Analysis*. London: Hogarth.